GREECE:

AMERICAN AID IN ACTION · 1947–1956

GREECE:

AMERICAN AID IN ACTION

1947 – 1956

BY WILLIAM HARDY McNEILL

THE TWENTIETH CENTURY FUND

NEW YORK · 1957

PHOTOGRAPH CREDITS: Acknowledgment is made to the following for permission to use the photographs which appear in this book:
United Nations: wartime refugees; road building; cement plant; farmers plowing. *Ebasco Services, Inc.:* power comes to a village; electric power station. *Royal Greek Embassy Information Service, Washington, D. C.:* nickel-processing plant; wheat harvesting. *Nellys Studios: cafeneion* in Crete; Salonika waterfront. *Mutual Security Agency:* women weeding rice fields.

*Manufactured in the United States of America
by Connecticut Printers, Incorporated, Hartford, Connecticut*

FOREWORD

In 1946 the Trustees of the Twentieth Century Fund focused their attention upon Greece as a crucial area in the developing world tension. That was before the declaration of the "Truman Doctrine" brought American support to replace the traditional British influence; well before Greece became an ally within NATO. A Twentieth Century Fund team visited the country, and *Report on the Greeks* by Frank Smothers, William Hardy McNeill and Elizabeth Darbishire McNeill was published by the Fund in 1948.

Eight years later, in the summer of 1956, Mr. McNeill was in a position to revisit Greece. It seemed useful to encourage him to bring up to date the earlier account. The present volume is in the nature of one man's attempt to see objectively but sympathetically the impact of American aid and of western policy upon a people at once variable and tenacious, blending old and new in a pattern uniquely its own.

In the nature of things, the end of the story cannot yet be told. Yet this interim record may help cast needed light. The foreign economic policies of the United States are being tested on a worldwide stage. The villages and towns of Greece provide one corner where experience has been gained — a corner that is by no means the least instructive, nor the least hopeful in its implications.

AUGUST HECKSCHER, *Director*
The Twentieth Century Fund

330 West 42 Street, New York
August 1957

ACKNOWLEDGMENTS

Without the willingness of literally hundreds of people in Greece to answer questions and search their records on my behalf, this little book could not have been written. The warmth and extravagant hospitality with which Greeks of every rank and station receive a stranger is, indeed, a source of never ending surprise to one accustomed to the atmosphere of an American city, and I wish hereby to thank all those, both friends and casual acquaintances, who thus contributed to my knowledge and understanding of the Greek scene.

More particularly, I owe a debt of gratitude to a number of busy officials of the Greek government who took time to talk with me, and more than once set wheels in motion to provide statistics and other special information I requested of them. In Salonika, Mr. Orphanides of the Agricultural Bank, and in Athens Mr. Leviratos of the Ministry of Coordination and Mr. Liakis of the National Statistical Services were especially helpful.

Among the members of the American community in Greece, I am particularly indebted to Mr. Bruce Lansdale, Director of the American Farm School in Salonika, and to Mr. Doggett of the aid mission. Mr. John Enepikides, of the American Embassy, also went far out of his way to help me find information I needed.

I must also gratefully acknowledge the assistance and friendship of Mr. John Skiriotis and Mr. John Boudouroglu, who made it possible for me to participate in the rapid fire of normal Greek conversation by translating my questions and interpreting the answers when I could not keep up with the pace.

Finally, the officers and staff of the Twentieth Century Fund contributed wisdom and careful scrutiny as well as money to the enterprise, and have caught at least some of my errors and inconsistencies before it was too late. For this, no less than for the grant that made my trip financially possible, I am the Fund's debtor.

Yet while all those whom I have named, as well as many personal friends in Greece whom I feel it best to leave anonymous, certainly helped to bring this book to birth, none of them is in the least responsible for the judgments and opinions I have expressed. Nor is the Twentieth Century Fund, in publishing this book, in any way committed to defend the accuracy of my analysis of Greek affairs. The final decision on matters of substance and emphasis was by necessity my own.

WILLIAM H. MC NEILL

CONTENTS

CONTENTS

THE COUNTRY
AND THE PEOPLE

Like other countries struggling under the impact of western technology and ideas, contemporary Greece is a land of sharp contrasts. Donkeys with loaded panniers on their backs still jog down the broad avenues of modern Athens oblivious to the stream of automobiles passing them by; and the donkeys' owners daily hawk their wares, with piercing and immemorial cries, to people living in ultra-modern apartment buildings, as well as to others who inhabit the merest hovels, clustered along narrow alleys behind the handsome main streets of the city. Similarly, in the countryside it is still possible to see groups of peasants toiling stoopbacked and patient as they harvest their grain with sickles, handful by handful, while, perhaps in the next field, an American combine may be observed noisily at work.

The combines and the glistening apartment buildings of Athens are very new; the donkeys and the sickles are older than recorded history. In a very real sense, the central problem of contemporary Greek life is how to close this gap, and bring the old and the new into a smooth and mutually beneficial interrelationship. Much progress has been made in this direction during the past ten years, but stubborn difficulties remain. It will require at least another generation before these difficulties can be overcome, even if peace and prosperity prevail throughout the coming years.

Peace and prosperity have seldom visited the Greeks for long, least of all during the twentieth century. Greece was almost continuously at war from 1912 to 1923 and again from 1940 to 1949; and the intervals of peace between these times of crisis were seldom secure. The wealth of the country suffered very severely from both periods of war, but in spite of economic dislocation and widespread destruction of property, the population increased fairly rapidly, from just over 5 million in 1920 (when Greece first attained approximately her present boundaries) to just about 8 million in 1956. Part of this growth was due to natural increase, but about one and a quarter million new inhabitants came to the country between 1922 and 1927, as a result of forcible exchanges of population with Turkey and Bulgaria after the first world war.

The effect of these exchanges was to make almost all of the population Greek in speech and sentiment, although two significant minority groups remained: a Slavic "Macedonian" population in the northwest where the borders of Greece, Yugoslavia and Albania come together, and a Turkish Moslem minority in Thrace. Official figures on the size of these minorities have not been published, but in all probability neither much exceeds 60,000 persons.

Greece is a small country, with a total area of slightly more than 50,000 square miles, or just about the size of the state of Illinois. It is also a poor country, lacking in any very important natural resources, short of fuel, but blessed with a magnificent climate similar to that of southern California. The country is very mountainous. Patches of fertile land, none of them very large, are separated from each other by tangles of barren hill and mountain. The main crops are wheat, grapes, olives, cotton and tobacco; and of these tobacco is by all odds the most important for foreign trade, since all the wheat and nearly all the cotton, wine and olive oil are consumed within the country, leaving only a surplus of tobacco, currants and a few other specialized agricultural products for export.

Industry is comparatively weak. Greek industrial exports have seldom been able to compete in price or quality on world markets. The Greek merchant marine, on the other hand, is one of the important fleets of the world; but many Greek-owned ships are not registered in Greece, and many of the most successful Greek shipowners do not live in the country of their birth. The reason is that Greek taxes on ships and shipowners are heavier than those levied by some other countries, and the shipowners therefore find it expedient to register their ships and take their profits elsewhere. They do, however, often recruit their crews in the home country, and thus offer a source of employment to several thousand Greeks.

Greece fought on the Allied side in both the first and second world wars, suffered German and Italian occupation between 1941 and 1944, and became a special British "sphere of influence" in political and military matters during 1944–46. Since

1946, United States influence has replaced British, and in 1951 Greece was admitted to the NATO alliance along with her neighbor, Turkey. Greece thus belongs to the free world, yet her geographical position, along one margin of the Communist heartland of eastern Europe, creates a constant threat to the nation's security.

Ever since the second world war the Greeks have therefore had to wrestle simultaneously with the problems of poverty and of political insecurity. Both were old problems in Greek history, but the scale was new — so much so that Greek resources were by themselves quite inadequate to meet the difficulties that loomed large after 1945. Only the delivery of substantial amounts of foreign, and especially of American, aid prevented political collapse and Communist revolution in the years just after the war.

This book will try to describe the successes and failures in this struggle, and make an estimate of the prospects for ultimate success in relieving poverty and improving social stability in Greece. Before launching on an account of what has been achieved, however, something should be said about the character of Greek society, with special attention to the points of difference that divide us in the United States from the Greeks.

Life in the Villages

The fundamental fact about Greece today is that in spite of the rather rapid growth of towns and cities in recent decades, the country still remains predominantly agrarian. In 1950, according to a special agricultural census, rural families comprised 4,770,783 persons, or 63 per cent of the estimated total population of the country in that year. Some of these families supplemented their agricultural income by seasonal employment in towns or on roads or other public works, and should, perhaps, not be counted as full-time farmers. Indeed, when one realizes that according to this same census the average family farm contained only a little more than 8 acres, and the amount of productive land per head of the rural population totaled just 1.75 acres, it is obvious that there are very few full-time farmers in Greece, if the term is taken to mean persons who busy themselves on the land throughout the year.

Except for a few weeks, when especially intensive work of cultivation or harvesting must be done, Greek peasant farmers enjoy a great deal of leisure, and spend it, characteristically, sitting in the village *cafeneion,* or coffee house, talking, playing backgammon, or just watching the passing scene. A casual observer might mistake such idleness for laziness; yet when tangible gain is to be won by working hard, Greek peasants do not spare themselves. But in practically every village there are far more hands than are needed to do the work of the fields; and when the needful work has been done, sitting in a coffee house is more entertaining than sitting at home. There a man may hear the latest gossip of the village, read the Athens newspapers, talk politics, and watch the shadows shift across the village square as the day progresses.

The women, on the other hand, lead a much harder life. Household tasks and the care of children take up most of the hours of the day, and in the seasons when field work is heavy, women work side by side with the men. For a woman to sit in a coffee house would be the grossest breach of etiquette, something quite unthinkable. The village water fountain may serve as a place for daily gossip; but it is the church which really provides the village women with a meeting place where they may on a Sunday morning, after (or even during) the service, talk and enjoy a few minutes of leisure each week. By a curious and unspoken law, the men of the villages usually do not attend church, save on feast days and other special occasions. Thus they avoid infringing on the women's meeting place, though not as rigorously as the women avoid the men's coffee house.

Nearly all villages conform to these customs, and much else unites them in a common pattern of life. Yet there is a very important distinction to be made between hill villages and villages of the plains. The distinction is not simply one of altitude. Hill villages, by and large, are located in areas so barren that the population cannot raise enough food for its own consumption, whereas plains villages, as would be expected, normally produce a food surplus for sale.

The traveler in Greece, especially if he leaves the main roads behind and explores some of the rough byways of the land, will frequently be surprised to find quite large villages perched in the most improbable places, hiding in some mountain cleft far from any substantial area of cultivable land. Equally surprising is the fact that in some of the broadest and most fertile plains, like that of Thessaly for instance, villages are rather widely separated. Places can be found where cultivated fields extend in all directions yet no house or village can be seen. In such localities, the fields are often tilled by peasants who live miles away in a village nestling in foothills near the margin of the plain.

The reason for this anomalous distribution of population is largely historical. In Turkish times, if not before, life in the plains was difficult and dangerous. Soldiers and officials, as they passed to and fro, lived off the local inhabitants. Tax and rent collectors, too, were more attentive to the plains dwellers, whose fields might be expected to produce more wealth for the collector to seize upon. These plagues were less serious in the back country, away from the main lines of communication. As a result, humble villagers found it safer to live in the hills, leaving the plains comparatively empty. But there was little food to be found in the uplands, and the Turkish landowners of the plains often needed extra hands to help cultivate their broad acres.

Hence a sort of symbiosis was established. A large proportion of the able-bodied men of the hill villages descended each year to the plains and worked in the fields of the Turkish landowners, then returned to their homes with wages, either in money or in kind, with which to supplement the produce of the tiny fields they had been able to carve from the mountain valleys and slopes around their homes.

Some of the hill villages developed occupational specialties, sending most of their able-bodied men each year to labor as masons or carpenters wherever work was to be found. Groups of villagers sometimes walked as much as a hundred miles to and from the scene of this sort of seasonal employment. Other villages developed what might be called industrial specialties — lime burning, rug weaving, wood carving and the like — and peddled their products far and wide during the summer season. One village even developed an international trade in specially dyed red wool and cloth during the latter years of the eighteenth century, stationing agents in such cities as Vienna, Constantinople and Leipzig. The origins of the modern Greek merchant marine were similar, for sailors were easily recruited among peasant boys of the islands and coasts, who sought seasonal employment to supplement what could be produced on the family farm.

Another pattern of migration should be mentioned, up into the higher mountain slopes rather than down to the plains. Each summer herds of sheep and goats were sent to pasture on the high ground, where vegetation stayed green through the summer drought, and then returned to lower altitudes when the snows fell. Quite a few hill villages specialized in sheepherding, accompanying their own sheep, and sometimes sheep entrusted to them by others as well, on this annual round.

As long as the hill villages lay between two relatively unpopulated geographic regions — the plains beneath and the peaks above — these complicated arrangements worked well enough. The Greek communities in the hills escaped the full rigor of Turkish oppression, maintained a very considerable degree of self-government, and were yet able to make a living by supplementing what they could produce in the immediate locality with what they could earn far afield.

Two other factors help to explain the concentration of population in the hills. One was water. Greece is a dry country in summer, and before modern well-drilling techniques were known, in many localities it was difficult or impossible to live the year around in the plains. A second factor was malaria. Until DDT came to Greece after the second world war, a very large part of the country was afflicted with chronic malaria. Hill valleys, where drainage was good, were often free of this disease when the plains were not.

Yet problems of water supply and the risk of malaria were not enough to keep eager Greek settlers from the fat lands of the plains when Turkish political control was withdrawn. On the contrary, as one region after another was liberated, between 1821 and 1913, Turkish landlords and peasants left or were driven out. Land so vacated was promptly settled by Greeks, many of whom came down from hill villages, while others came from Asia Minor in 1922 and 1923, fleeing the wrath of Turkish armies. Only in western Thrace was the Turkish peasantry allowed to remain on the land in return for a guarantee from Turkey not to disturb the Greek inhabitants of Constantinople and eastern Thrace.

But what would happen when the Turks had been driven from the scene, and the plains had been pre-empted by Greek peasant communities? Clearly, this development, however satisfying to national sentiments, spelled growing hardship for those who remained behind in the ancient hill villages. A landlord with hundreds or thousands of acres might be eager to hire large numbers of men to help till his ground for him; a peasant farmer, owning thirty or forty acres, needed comparatively little outside help with his crops. Moreover, as the population of the plains villages grew, farms were subdivided, and there was less and less need of outside labor. Thus the old symbiosis between hill and plain was upset as the plains came to be more densely occupied by a peasant farming population. The hillsmen, whose numbers continued to increase, had to seek new outlets.

The major outlet they discovered was emigration overseas, especially to the United States. This was, in a sense, merely a geographic extension of the familiar pattern of going away from home to seek work. Largely for this reason, many of the Greek emigrants who came to this country — mainly between 1900 and 1924 — arrived with no intention of remaining permanently in their new environment. They hoped instead to make enough money to allow them to go back home to their village, and there buy a house and some land in order to live in the traditional style of their forefathers. Many of course stayed, finding the new life overseas more satisfactory than the old one at home; but many thousands acted upon their original plans and returned. As a result, even today when an American arrives in one of the remoter and more isolated villages of Greece, it is no uncommon thing to be met by some returned migrant who spent the best years of his youth in Chicago or New York, and can produce a few words of broken English to prove it. Richer villages in the plains, on the contrary, seldom sent men overseas. As long as the family enjoyed enough land to be able to live in the simple style to which the Greek peasants were accustomed, there was no compelling motive that would lead a man to undertake such a perilous and expensive venture.

In 1924 the United States established a quota on immigration which virtually stopped the stream of Greek migration to this country. At about the same time, most of the other countries of

the world that could offer an attractive chance to an impecuni-
ous peasant boy also put legal barriers in the way, so that this
escape from the deteriorating position of the hill villages of
Greece was rather abruptly cut off.

Within Greece, the growth of towns and a modest development of industry, which scarcely antedated the 1920's, offered
an escape for a few of the surplus hands that had appeared in
the hill villages. But this was by no means adequate to take care
of the problem. Not only was the growth of industry and urban
occupations comparatively slow, while the rate at which the
peasant population grew was high, but even more important,
in 1922 and 1923 Greece was compelled to accommodate more
than a million refugees from Asia Minor — people who had
been uprooted from their homes by the Turks as a consequence
of the war between Greece and Turkey which lasted from 1920
to 1922. Many of these refugees had followed urban occupations in Asia Minor, and clustered naturally in the larger cities
of Greece, where their skills and entrepreneurial energy frequently opened paths to them which were closed to the ordinary Greek peasant seeking employment away from home.

It was therefore not surprising that Greek peasants, especially
those cooped up in hill villages, exhibited a growing distress
and bafflement during the 1920's and 1930's, since their traditional patterns of life no longer sufficed to bring wonted results.
The world depression of the 1930's hit Greece hard, and contributed to the collapse of parliamentary government in 1936,
when General John Metaxas established a dictatorship. Metaxas
attempted to relieve the economic problems of the country by
launching an ambitious program of public works, especially
road building; and the expansion of the army and gendarmerie
which he carried through also afforded careers to a number of
young men from poor hill villages. But this was palliative rather
than cure. When the second world war came, followed by Ital-

ian and German occupation and drastic derangement of the national economy, the situation of the hill villages became truly desperate. Starvation visited many of them.

Famine in time of war was age-old; and the response of the hillsmen of Greece also had very ancient precedent behind it, for they took gun in hand, and attempted to seize forcibly what they could no longer gain peaceably from the plains. They formed the backbone of the wartime resistance forces, and justified their violence by patriotism, quite in the spirit their forefathers had shown in attacking the Turks. Yet the resistance movement was not merely a reassertion of old patterns. Its leadership was mainly provided by Communists, who in earlier years had been a small and not very significant group, largely confined to the towns. [1]

In the wartime resistance movement the inhabitants of the hill villages found a sort of economic relief, inasmuch as the guerrilla bands lived by raiding the plains, taking by force a part of the agricultural surplus of those regions in order to feed themselves. A young man, without any real occupation in his native village, and without any hope of a career at home which could satisfy even the traditionally low level of expectation among the hillsmen, could, by joining a guerrilla band, hope to feed himself and relieve his family of the burden of his presence. In addition, he could become a hero, fighting for freedom and liberty, social justice and a better life for all.

For most peasant boys, the ulterior aims of their Communist leaders meant little or nothing. Indeed, the Communists were at very considerable pains to play down any plans they had for social revolution, and welcomed persons of widely differing social views into the ranks of the resistance. This was, of course,

1. There were a number of non-Communist resistance bands also, but most of them did not last long, and the successful ones were confined to Epirus, in the northwest.

thoroughly in harmony with the "popular front" tactics incul-
cated by international Communist policy. When British intervention in 1944 prevented the resistance forces from seizing
power in Greece, the rank and file of those who had supported
the Communists during the war had little reason to distrust
their leaders, since the Communists had not had time or opportunity to carry through the revolution they hoped for.

As a result, when in 1946 international Communist policy
again mobilized the energies of the Greek Communist party to
begin a new guerrilla war, Communist organizers found little
difficulty in winning the sympathy and support of the same social groups that had participated in the wartime resistance
movement. The hill villages were prepared to send their young
men into the guerrilla ranks for the same reasons as before. Liberation had not brought prosperity, and without prosperity in
the cities and plains, life in the hills was very hard. Hence the
Communists found it easy to create guerrilla bands in all the
mountainous regions of the country.

In the most obvious sense, both of these recent guerrilla
movements failed. Their leaders were killed or driven from the
country, and the government remained in other hands. Yet in
another sense, it must be recognized that the imprint of the two
guerrilla enterprises upon the attitudes of the hill villages of
Greece has been deep, and seems likely to last a long time.

Basically, what the Communists achieved was to convince
nearly everyone in the villages that the traditional way of living was no longer even to be wished for and striven after. Instead, they held out fascinating and quite unrealizable dreams
of bathtubs and electric refrigerators for all. Or rather, they
held this out as an ultimate goal, and offered in the more immediate future a life of activity, violence and dedication — a
life that at least seemed to have significance and purpose and
hope. These were just what the average young man or woman

in the hill villages (and in only slightly less degree the other young people of Greece also) lacked, yet desperately needed in order to confront the daily hardships and disappointments of private life. Here, I think, lay and continues to lie the secret of Communist influence in Greece. It was not so much the ultimate vision of wealth and ease and justice — Greek peasants are quite sophisticated enough to distrust such glittering baubles — but the mobilization of energies in the here and now to form a purposeful movement, surcharged with hope and optimism, that attracted the allegiance of so many restless young people.

At the least it seems correct to say that the guerrilla movements, with their attendant propaganda and real life experiences, created a population more or less chronically open to fresh revolutionary winds, from whatever direction they may blow. Even when jobs on roads and other sorts of construction opened up again in the 1950's, so that something resembling the old symbiosis of hill and plains could be resumed, the changed attitudes among the hillsmen remained quite obvious. Greece will have, for some considerable time to come, a substantial group of its population that is peculiarly receptive to movements of political dissent or outright revolution.

The real, physical problems presented by too many mouths and too little land have not been solved, and cannot be solved quickly by anything short of wholesale depopulation. But the tradition-bound attitudes which once made this precarious life seem inevitable, even if not right, have been profoundly eroded. Clearly, this is a dangerous and potentially explosive situation. What happens in the hill villages is likely to constitute the critical factor in the future political history of Greece.

The situation in the plains was different. Guerrilla bands seemed suspiciously like robbers, or at best like tax collectors, to the peasants of the plains villages from whom they demanded food. Comparatively few young men left such villages to join the guerrillas, even in the south, where landless families existed in many plains communities. The hard times that drove the hillsmen from home, gun in hand, impelled the plainsmen to stay home where there was food. More recently, the revival and improvement of agriculture naturally proceeded furthest and fastest in regions where the soil was reasonably fertile and abundant. Hence, the plains villagers have been able to achieve far better results than the hillsmen from technical and marketing changes. They have property and social status to defend, and know quite enough about Communist agrarian policy in neighboring countries to distrust beguiling words from Communist lips.

The farmers of the plains are therefore not revolutionary, even though they may grumble about present hardship, and envy others better off than themselves. They have seen quite enough of the violence and suffering which revolutions, or attempted revolutions, involve. The hillsmen, too, have suffered, and do not love violence for its own sake. But, unless I am much mistaken, they remain potential revolutionaries.

Town Life

Just as the combine and the sickle join in uneasy partnership to harvest the wheat fields of Greece, so also in the towns an age-old style of life is set side by side with a few completely up-to-date factories and the most modern urban amenities. The juxtaposition in an urban context is no less awkward than in the country.

Particularly in the north, where Turkish times are still within living memory, in towns like Jannina or Kozani, one can see streets where artisans pursue their trades in little shops just as their predecessors have done for centuries. The old medieval principle still holds, whereby shops dealing in the same goods cluster together, so that one may find whole rows of silver-smiths' shops in Jannina, or streets of cobblers in Kozani. The market square, where peasants from the surrounding villages bring their products for sale once or twice a week, constitutes a vital part of every town; street peddlers with their donkeys or pushcarts are everywhere. So are policemen, shoeshine boys and waiters, who will bring little cups of Turkish coffee into any office or house when summoned from the ubiquitous *cafeneions*. Great trucks and buses, often sadly dilapidated, are a prominent part of the urban scene, and, except in Athens, they outnumber passenger cars.

The daily rhythm of life in a Greek town is quite different from that familiar in the United States. People rise early, almost with the sun, and the streets in the early morning present a lively scene, as the women buy food and other household supplies and men start their daily work. As the sun mounts the sky, the streets become more deserted, until in early afternoon only a few idlers can be seen hugging the shade in the coffee shops or along the curbs. Shops close and everyone goes home to eat and sleep. By late afternoon animation returns, though it is less intense than in the morning, since many offices (including government offices) function only until early afternoon. Then with the cool of the day, about 7:30 or 8 o'clock, the streets come fully to life. Everyone who can walk comes out for a breath of air. Dense crowds move slowly through the center of town, talking and window shopping. In the main square, the young people form small groups and walk round and round, the boys in one direction and the girls in the other, thus assuring each a maximum opportunity to observe, ogle or snub the opposite sex. This is how courtship begins, and the process lends a certain vivacity to the evening. Then, by 9:30 or so, everyone goes home, lights go out and the town goes to sleep until the morrow's sunrise.

Even in Athens-Piraeus this pattern is observed in many of the neighborhoods into which the two cities divide. The majority of Athenians live in suburbs which date back only to 1923 and the years immediately after, when tens of thousands of refugees from Asia Minor crowded into the town. Many of these communities have a strong corporate sense of their own, and live in much the same way as the smaller provincial towns already described. In the central part of Athens, however, life pursues a rhythm more or less like that of any big European city except that here, too, the midday siesta is rigorously observed. Also, new suburbs, inhabited by professional people and employees, have in recent years grown up farther from the center of town; here little of the community spirit of the older suburbs is to be found, and life rather resembles the dormitory belt of a big American city.

The superabundant leisure so characteristic of village life is also apparent in the towns. *Cafeneions* are numerous and nearly always the sidewalk tables are well filled with men who obviously have no pressing business, if indeed they have any business at all. Street corners, curbs and squares are also occupied by the poor, who cannot afford to pay for a seat by ordering a coffee, even though a modest 2½ drachmae (7 cents) will confer title to a table for an entire morning.

Every considerable town has a fringe of unemployed and semi-employed inhabitants, many of them migrants from villages who have come seeking some sort of job to supplement the inadequate income from their family farms. Such persons can always go back to the village if need be, where at least they can have a roof over their heads and something to eat. Even when a man has been successful in finding regular employment in a town, and makes his home there, he often continues to maintain a connection with the village from which he, or his father or grandfather, came. Family ties are very strong in

Greece, far more so than in the United States, so that a cousin or uncle who has set himself up in town will expect to help his relatives to find a footing in town when they attempt to make the escape from the land, and will also expect to be received back into the family if dire necessity should ever compel him to abandon his town career. Family ties of this sort provide a bond between town and country, extending to the second or even the third generation.

The psychological relationship between town and country is, however, subtle and complex. A peasant regards a man who has no land as something less than a full man; at the same time, most peasants envy what they feel to be the easier, richer and more stimulating life led by townsfolk, and especially by Athenians. Town dwellers, characteristically, regard themselves as far more intelligent, better informed and more civilized than the peasants. Yet elements of peasant outlook still survive among them, particularly the burning desire to own a house and a bit of land on which to plant a grape arbor and raise flowers or a few vegetables.

In town a man's most important relations are with outsiders, while in the village, relations within the family and a circle of relatives dominate daily life. In town, people must buy and sell every day, and the market relationship is shot through with antagonism, since it appears that in any immediate situation one party's gain is the other's loss. Prolonged bargaining — typical of any purchase, even of vegetables in the street — expresses this attitude; and the chicanery and high markups generally characteristic of Greek business are a consequence of the same spirit which sees in any outsider a legitimate victim, to be fleeced if possible. In village life, where market relations are merely occasional, mutual help and cooperation within the family circle provide the matrix of daily living. To be sure, outside the family circle, Greek peasants can be just as ruthless as

Greek townspeople; the difference is that townsmen must deal constantly with outsiders, whereas the peasants do so only occasionally.

This contrast lends a profoundly different timbre to town as against village life. In the countryside, a foreigner is treated as an honored family guest, and is often hard put to it to avoid abusing the hospitality of people who can ill afford to be generous. In towns, also, a foreigner is courteously received, but he will be cheated in small ways all the time. Prices tend to double when he appears on the scene, and if his tips, for services real or imaginary, are not far above the ordinary Greek level, he will be made to feel stingy.

Another marked characteristic of Greek town life is the sharpness of the line drawn between the manual and non-manual occupations. A secondary school education is the open sesame to a white-collar job, and a man who has achieved that level of education will not dirty his hands if he can help it. Otherwise he would seem to surrender the status so hard-won by his years in school. One consequence of this attitude is that skilled workmen and technicians are sometimes hard to find. Anyone in a position to afford an education will try for an academic course, preparing him for the white-collar class; a technical education which could only perpetuate a close connection with machinery and manual labor simply does not appeal to an ambitious boy. Even engineers are very prone to prefer a desk job to work in the field; and in the field they not infrequently dress in city clothes and supervise from a distance, where mud and other unpleasantnesses can be avoided. There are signs that these attitudes are weakening in the younger generation, but they are still very strong.

The disdain for manual labor is perhaps part of a more general social scheme of values which puts the rentier at or near the top of the social pyramid. To own land or buildings that will produce an income without personal effort is for most Greeks the pinnacle of ambition; and those who fall short of this ideal but still manage to escape the necessity of manual work sometimes allow the nail of the little finger on one hand to grow long as public proof of their privileged status.

Most Greek towns are predominantly commercial centers. Small shops, run by the members of a single family, are far more typical than any larger enterprise. There is a tremendous proliferation of independent entrepreneurs, working often on a shoestring. Even the employees of a larger concern are very likely to dabble on the side in buying or selling some commodity or service, partly because wages and salaries are low and hours are short, but partly also because no Greek really likes to work for someone else if he can possibly work for himself.

This phenomenon is intimately connected with the tight-knit character of Greek families. The members of a family group are ready and willing to work hard for the common benefit, and can usually arrange for a distribution of the profits among themselves without undue quarreling. But a man employed by an outsider, bound to him by no family ties, finds it hard not to feel that he is being exploited. Why should a stranger hire him if not to make something out of him? And why, then, should an employee not do his best to look after himself first and foremost, help his family and relatives next, and let the interests of the larger enterprise in which he is a mere hired hand take a poor third place in his loyalties?

The result is that when enterprises grow large, and employ persons not bound together by family relationships, they tend to lose much of the efficiency and esprit de corps of the small family undertaking. Nepotism and other forms of special favors done for relatives creep in. Given the strength of Greek family ties, promotion by the cold-blooded criterion of the individual's usefulness to an impersonal organization can scarcely prevail against the clamorous demands of deserving relatives who badly need a job.

The strong egalitarian spirit that runs through Greek life works in a somewhat parallel fashion to undermine the efficiency of large concerns. When every man feels himself just as good as everybody else, personal loyalty to a superior in a bureaucratic organization is difficult to establish. A bold spirit is sorely tempted to launch some sort of petty intrigue against his immediate boss, in the hope of displacing him and perhaps inheriting the position. More cautious persons are prone to develop a false servility and flattery of their superiors, in the hope of winning special confidence and favor. Both attitudes interfere with the effectiveness of large-scale organization; and both arise in large part from the underlying distrust Greeks feel toward anyone outside the sacred circle of the family.

Observations such as these are, of course, impressionistic, and it is not difficult to find many exceptions to the rule. Yet no one can deny that petty intrigue, nepotism and a remarkably ruthless pursuit of individual self-interest are far more widespread in Greece than in more industrially advanced countries. Indeed, these psychological characteristics of the Greek people perhaps have much to do with the relatively backward state of their technology, quite apart from the financial and physical difficulties which also hinder the development of large-scale modern industry in the country. Modern technology is, after all, incompatible with small-scale family enterprise; cooperation of larger numbers of men is necessary, and the traditions of the Greek people make such cooperation difficult to achieve.

This psychological attitude clearly makes the position of wage and salary earners less satisfactory than it might otherwise be. Anyone who has had any contact with the fierce intrigue that often disfigures personal relations among a group of Greek employees is likely to wonder how men can endure such tensions, only to remember how precious a job is to every Greek, and how impossible it is for a man to throw up a position in disgust in the hope of finding another and better one. There are, however, other factors which make the position of wage and salary earners difficult, and foster chronic discontent among them.

Wages are low, and are constantly in danger of being undercut by young men coming from the villages in search of work. Such new arrivals can often afford to work for less than a regular urban resident, for they have no homes or families to maintain, and can, in summer at least, sleep outdoors and eat very little in order to save a small sum with which to return home in the fall. As a result, a large part of the building trades, for example, is in the hands of migrant labor. Unions can do little to improve wages or working conditions when dozens of applicants seek every job that opens, and are ready, if need be, to bid against one another in order to get employment at all. Moreover, the prestige accorded to white-collar work and to immunity from manual toil obviously puts the working class at a psychological disadvantage, and builds up a sense of grievance among those condemned to labor with their hands.

Like the hill villagers, the workingmen of the towns were deeply infiltrated by Communist propaganda during the second world war. Attacks upon the rich, as traitors to the nation and oppressors of the poor, won widespread response. And indeed, the conduct of the small group of wealthy men in Greece lent some color to the accusations which Communists launched against them. Most men of property felt it more vital to safeguard their possessions than to join in any active resistance to the German and Italian authorities. Many of them exhibited the same ruthlessness against everyone beyond the family circle that most Greeks exhibit, and did so even when people were actually starving in the streets, as they were in 1941. Acts of generosity and kindliness did something to redeem the balance, but were comparatively rare. The wealthy classes did not, as a rule, show much sign of social conscience or sense of obligation to the poor. Once again, the solidarity and exclusiveness of family sentiment interfered with larger loyalties and sympathies. The result was that antagonism between rich and poor broke out into the open during the war years, and has never since ceased to trouble the political stability of the country.

Economic conditions have been acting, for at least fifteen years, to sharpen this feeling. Since 1941 Greece has experienced a series of monetary inflations that raised prices, sometimes rapidly, sometimes more slowly, but always faster than adjustments were made in wage and salary scales. As prices outran wages, workingmen faced a series of crises, the more serious because their wage rates were low to begin with. Adjustments of wages, when they came, relieved the problem only temporarily until continuing inflation once again robbed the currency of part of its purchasing power.

The economic plight of white-collar employees was nearly the same as that of manual workingmen, for they, too, had to live on an income that regularly lagged behind the price level. Moreover, the fact that such persons had gone to school, and therefore felt they had a rightful claim to superior social status, did not make it easier for them to face a life of poverty. The fierce struggle to win a place in the government civil service was only matched by the chronic discontent of those who had succeeded in getting government jobs and then found that they could scarcely live on their salaries.

Fortunately for the political stability of the country, wage earners and salaried classes are a minority in Greece. This is no more than a corollary of the small size and family character of most Greek economic undertakings. Nevertheless, if one adds the hillsmen of the countryside as a third more or less chronically disaffected class, there emerges a formidable grouping of unstable and potentially revolutionary elements in present-day Greek society. The more conservative groups — farmers of the plains villages, shopkeepers, traders and property owners in the towns, and the handful of rich shipowners and other large capitalists — certainly outweigh the dissidents in normal times. But times have seldom been normal in recent Greek history, and the balance of forces has not uniformly inclined in favor of the established social order.

Public Life in 1947

The winter and spring of 1946–47 were months when the balance turned strongly against conservatism. As a matter of fact, Greece seemed then to teeter on the verge of Communist revolution. The Greek Communist party, acting in concert with the Communist governments and parties of neighboring countries to the north, and with the approval or perhaps under the instructions of the Russians, began to raise guerrilla bands in the mountains of Greece in the summer of 1946. Organizers met with rather quick response in many hill villages, where the young men and boys were stewing in their discontent and welcomed the high hopes held out to them by Communist promises. The national army was quite unable to check the spread of the guerrilla movement. For one thing, morale was uncertain. Many soldiers felt strong distaste for fighting fellow Greeks. When sallies were made from strong points which the army had constructed, the guerrillas simply melted away, only to reappear a few days later somewhere else, soon to return to the same district as before.

The morale of the government was equally uncertain. Communist lands were very near; Britain was embarrassed by financial difficulties; the United States was far away. No one was sure that aid would come, or if it came that it would arrive soon enough and in large enough quantity to turn the tide. Yet foreign aid was clearly needed if the Communist guerrillas were to be stopped. Without it, the government could scarcely hope to maintain its army for long. More than that, the fabric of the civil economy could not stand by itself, especially when guerrilla raids and road mines made transport and communication unsafe.

Apart from the military and diplomatic aspects, there was another and more fundamental sense in which the morale of the government and of the conservative classes was damaged. The general ideas and presuppositions of the non-Communist politicians and their supporters were badly shaken by the course of events in the immediate postwar period. Their general assumption had been that once the Germans had withdrawn and a transition period of special emergency had been passed through, then the society and economy of Greece would return of themselves to something like stability and the prewar pattern. Yet now the Germans had departed, UNRRA had come and gone (save for a small rear guard), and still there was no stability and no security. Far less was there any prospect of prosperity.

The upheaval of the war years had in fact been too drastic to permit any automatic return to normal. But the political leaders of the country, all of whom had grown up in a world where government economic policy and administration were conceived in terms of doing favors for one's friends and withholding them from one's opponents, had no idea how to cope with the disturbed and unhappy society entrusted to their guidance. No idea, that is, except to ask for help from Britain or the United States.

The politicians could scarcely be accused of not having done their part to bring things back to normal. During the brief respite between the time when British troops had suppressed the wartime guerrilla army in December 1944, and the resumption of the guerrilla war in the summer of 1946, the politicians resumed the prewar game of politics with an exemplary faithfulness to old customs and methods. Two of the principal figures of Greek politics, Sophocles Venizelos and Constantine Tsaldaris, carried family names that had been illustrious in the twenties and thirties, and owed their leadership more to their names than to any personal attributes. Quarrels between royalists and republicans, which dated back to the first world war, remained the principal line of demarcation between rival groups of politicians; and demands for territorial expansion at the expense of the defeated powers — primarily Bulgaria — remained a major stock-in-trade of political oratory, and the best antidote the political leaders could find for the discontent and unrest of the nation. This, after all, had been the dominant theme in the career of the great Eleftherios Venizelos, who had almost doubled Greek territory between 1912 and 1919, and even for a dizzy moment seemed to have the old Byzantine capital of Constantinople within his grasp. And how could any politician hope to improve on Venizelist models?

Fame and fortune had always been the stuff and substance of a political career; special favors to friends and supporters had always been the means by which power was sustained; parties had always been fragile coalitions of ambitious public men who combined for a longer or shorter time under the leadership of one of their number, only to scatter and re-form in some new constellation when the restless striving for place and position dictated a change.

To be sure, even before the war, extensive social legislation had been enacted, and the idea that the government was somehow responsible for maintaining the welfare of the population at large was not unknown. But such measures were conceived primarily as electoral maneuvers, aimed to win votes, rather than as aspects of any general social policy. A managed economy, or even a semi-managed economy, in which government decisions influenced the flow and volume of investment, regulated the supply of money, and adjusted the share of the national income to be enjoyed by different groups in the population was scarcely within the purview of the old-style politicians. Once again, this was not because the government had not intervened repeatedly and with telling effect in the economic life of the country. It had, but usually in the spirit of helping political or personal friends and thwarting foes.

Yet in spite of the faithful and unimaginative efforts of the political cosmos (the name Greeks give to the small number of men who play leading roles in political life) to return to a comfortable prewar pattern of behavior, the country ungratefully failed to follow suit. The times remained desperately out of joint, but knowing no way to set them right, the conservative politicians and their supporters were in a quandary. Their morale was destroyed by the lack of any clearly defined and firmly felt purpose and program, quite as much as by the diplomatic and material difficulties they confronted. Among the men of the right, apathy and hopelessness alternated with sporadic anti-Communist and extra-legal violence; but neither the one nor the other seemed to do anything but make the situation worse.

The Greek Communist party was not without its own internal difficulties, but by comparison with the old-style politicians the Communists had tremendous advantages. First and foremost, they commanded a disciplined, enthusiastic and energetic body of committed followers, men who could be counted upon to follow instructions and who were willing to undergo personal hardship in the service of their dream for the future. Beyond this, the Communists enjoyed the sympathy or admiration of a considerable proportion of the population, especially among the workmen of the towns and the peasants of the hill villages. No one can say how large this group was, but to estimate it at about 20 per cent of the nation's total population is a reasonable guess.

Another important asset of the Communists was their wartime record as leaders of resistance against the Germans and Italians. They could plausibly paint themselves as true champions of Greek national freedom and of democracy, while accusing their opponents of betraying the interests of the nation first to the Axis and then to the British. To be both a patriot and a Communist sympathizer did not therefore seem incompatible.

Finally, and perhaps most important of all, the Communists did have a more or less definite program of action and knew what they wanted. They were able to explain the continued distress of the country as a natural result of the creeping crisis of capitalism. They had a ready cure at hand in the abolition of private ownership of the means of production, as a preliminary to planned industrial expansion, on the Russian model. To many Communist followers, no doubt, the program meant little more than an angry intention to take from the rich and give to the poor, i.e., to themselves, all the good things which had selfishly and unjustly been withheld from them. Others, more sophisticated, realized that there would inevitably be a long period of time when suffering and poverty still would prevail, but believed that in the long run the dream of abundance for all could be realized, if the government planned economic activity and compelled sufficient investment. And no matter what the degree of economic understanding among their followers, the Communists had the advantage of offering the distressed and confused a cause to which to dedicate themselves, an enemy against whom to fight, and a hope for the future. None of the old-line political parties or leaders could do any of these things nearly so effectively.

Only the inner circle of the Greek Communist party was directly affected by the very real fissure between what may be called "home grown" and "Russian" Communists. The rank and file of party members and sympathizers were perhaps scarcely aware of any such tensions, and accepted without any special notice the transfer of authority over the Greek Communist party from the hands of George Siantos, who had led it during the war years, to those of Nicholas Zachariades, who had spent the war in a German concentration camp. Yet this shift, accomplished in May 1945, represented the assertion of control by leaders trained and directed by Moscow, as against the more independent "home grown" leadership which Siantos had embodied.

In any case, this fissure was only of potential importance. If Russian policy should diverge seriously from lines acceptable to "home grown" Communists, then the factions in the Greek Communist party might be expected to come into the open. So long as no such divergence appeared — and in 1946 and 1947 it did not — the only consequence was to elevate some persons to positions of authority in the party and to blight the careers of others who had thrown in their lot with the defeated side.

Hence, in 1946 and 1947 the advantages enjoyed by the Greek Communist party in competition with its rivals were actual, its weaknesses only potential. This was true not only within the country, but internationally as well. The Communist countries to the north began actively assisting the Greek Communist bands, sending arms and ammunition, allowing hard-pressed units to find refuge across the border, and providing hospital and other services to them as far as geographical difficulties permitted. On the other hand, British military and economic support for the Greek government was about to be withdrawn, and it was not yet clear that American support would be forthcoming to replace the British. Under the circumstances it is not strange that the Communists went from strength to strength, while their opponents were filled with foreboding for the future.

To be sure, the Communists faced one great obstacle. Their opponents were still in full control of the administrative machine of government. The pattern so successfully followed in eastern European countries which fell within the Russian sphere of influence, whereby Communists first acquired a toehold in the administration and then used their position to push all rivals out, could scarcely be employed in Greece. The police, army and civil bureaucracy were all firmly in anti-Communist hands. British armed intervention in 1944 had been necessary to secure this state of affairs, but it was confirmed by elections held in 1946; and the new aggressiveness of international Communist policies did not permit patient waiting until some future election might lead to a coalition including Communist ministers.

Yet the effectiveness of these instruments of power was sadly blunted in Greece. In the countryside the police were too few to resist concerted attack by guerrilla bands. The army was numerous enough, but the morale of the soldiers made offensive actions against the guerrillas difficult and largely ineffective. The civil bureaucracy was distinguished by its clumsiness and occasional corruption. Efforts to prevent corruption led to excessive centralization, so that even simple decisions had constantly to be referred to Athens, and not infrequently to a cabinet member, before action could be taken. The nomarchs, the principal local officials in the provinces, characteristically spent more time in Athens, haunting the central offices of the government in hope of getting needed decisions, money or supplies, than they did in the districts assigned to them. Incidentally, of course, they could thereby consolidate personal relations with higher authority, promote their own careers, and enjoy the amenities of Athenian existence. But in the meantime much that should have been done remained undone.

Senior officials and ministers were harrassed by incredible numbers of papers requiring their signature or countersignature; they were harrassed even more by the crowds of petitioners who stood outside every door and not infrequently pushed their way inside to watch for a chance to seize the great man's attention. Subordinates, on the other hand, seldom would or could take any initiative themselves, but referred everything to higher authority, where the papers added to the jam at the top.

Perhaps the greatest weakness of the whole system was that officialdom shared the intellectual and technical deficiencies of the politicians. In the general confusion and pressure of daily business, no one had time or opportunity to try to think in long terms, measure the economic and other needs of the country, and attempt to establish some sort of priority among them, so that a beginning, however modest, could be made toward repairing some of the disbalances and defects of Greek society. Perhaps the magnitude of the problems and the sheer inadequacy of Greek resources to cope with most of them made such calculations impracticable. But it was also true that the officials of the Greek government were not accustomed to thinking in such terms, and tended to assume that problems of this nature should be left to solve themselves by the spontaneous action of private citizens, within the framework of traditional patterns of living. In proportion as the physical and psychological basis of such a traditional framework had been destroyed by the war, this assumption was no longer valid; but few, indeed, in the turmoil of the civil administration realized this fact, and fewer were ready, intellectually or morally, to try to move into the gaps thus created in the social structure, and attempt to put the scattered fragments back into some sort of working order.

Under the circumstances, then, nothing like an efficient administration confronted the Communist challenge. Private citizens, who were unable to get satisfaction from officials, even when they knew their claims were right and just, were not encouraged to feel any special loyalty to the regime; and a government which was able to do so little to remedy the general disorganization of economic and social life gave color to the Communists' claim that they and they alone could solve the country's problems.

There were, nevertheless, some persons who were attempting to devise plans for the economic and social stabilization of the country. Some held government positions, some were unemployed or semi-employed engineers and the like. Perhaps the most influential circle was that associated with the UNRRA Mission to Greece, which, in addition to delivering relief supplies to the country, had attempted to rehabilitate the nation as well. The time and the funds allocated to UNRRA proved grossly inadequate to rehabilitate Greece, but studies and plans made by UNRRA, to discover what could and should be done to put the country back on its feet, had at least the virtue of turning some men's minds to the long-term problem. Some of these plans, and some of the personnel that helped draw them up, later played a part in the United States aid program.

Apart from this historical connection, one can say that even in the darkest days of 1947, when Communist victory seemed far from improbable, there did exist on the fringes of Greek official life a small number of persons who had begun to think in terms that might effectively meet the Communist challenge. Planners and statisticians, engineers and economists — men who conceived the task of the government to include efforts to shape economic and social development in such a fashion as to relieve the poverty of the nation — did exist. They were, however, far removed from the real centers of power and authority in the government. Unassisted, they would certainly not have been able to do anything effective to overcome the Communist menace.

To sum up: The nature of Greek society and the shortcomings of the Greek government, together with the constellation of international relations in 1946 and 1947, made Communist revolution possible, indeed probable. But the injection of a massive new force, United States aid, changed the direction of events and prevented that consummation. The activity of the American aid missions will therefore be the subject of the next chapter.

CHAPTER 2

AMERICAN AID

The Economic and Political Scene in 1947

As a result of wartime agreements between the three great allied powers, Greece was recognized as a British "sphere of influence" in the immediate postwar period. In December 1944, less than two months after the end of the German occupation, British troops intervened to defeat ELAS, the Communist-led wartime resistance army, and British advice did much to shape the policy of the Greek government in the days that followed. In particular, British funds and personnel were made available to organize, train and equip a Greek army and gendarmerie. By the beginning of 1947, however, the British government decided that it could no longer pay the costs involved, and privately informed the United States that future British budgets would no longer carry any provision for aid to Greece.

The Greek civilian economy was in no condition to sustain the armed forces which had been built up with British aid. On the contrary, it, too, was dependent on foreign funds which had come through UNRRA. But UNRRA operations were scheduled to come to a close at the end of March 1947. Hence it became clear to President Truman and his advisers that Greece was heading for a sudden and drastic collapse unless the United States decided to step into the breach and continue the aid programs started by UNRRA and the British. Nor could there be any doubt as to who would profit from such a collapse. In the mountains of northern Greece, Communist-led guerrilla bands were already in the field, and in the towns and cities of the country, Communist newspapers and agitators carried on a scarcely less effective war of words against the Greek government.

Greece was far away from the United States, and in times past the eastern Mediterranean had scarcely been a region of serious concern to Americans. American newspapers and officials had been generally critical of British intervention in Greece in 1944, and in the months that followed they found little to praise in the conduct of the Greek government. But the prospect of a Communist Greece, outflanking an already hard-pressed Turkey, and opening the Mediterranean to the Soviet bloc, could not be taken lightly.

This was the situation which led President Truman, on March 12, 1947, to go before Congress and ask the allocation of $400 million for aid to Greece and Turkey. The "cold war" was then still a novelty, and American opinion was not yet fully convinced that the United States should take the lead in checking the spread of Communism all around the world. Hence the debate on President Truman's proposal was lengthy and serious, both in and out of Congress; but in the end, in May 1947, Congress voted to approve the aid. This decision marked a fundamental turning point in postwar American foreign policy; it marked an even more decisive turning point in Greek affairs, since the prospect of American aid staved off the threatened collapse of the Greek government, and its arrival eventually turned the tide against the Communists.

The first shipments of military and civilian supplies from the United States under the Truman program did not reach Greece until August 1947. In the meantime, two important changes came to Greece. First, United States officials negotiated a series of agreements to define the rights and powers which would be possessed by American personnel sent to supervise the use made of American funds and materials. These agreements gave very wide authority to American representatives, so much so that the Greek government itself was thenceforth unable to take any important decision without their approval. At the time there was little objection. The Greeks knew they needed help, and were not inclined to quibble over details.

The second change was more subtle but even more important. From March 1947, when President Truman first asked for American intervention in Greece, until July, Communist policy remained ambiguous. On the one hand, guerrilla bands in the hills were waging war against the Greek government under the leadership of subordinate and therefore relatively inconspicuous Communists. At the same time, the top leadership of the party remained "legal," though often in hiding. It seems clear that the men at the top hoped political negotiation might bring them into a Greek cabinet, from which position, seizure of power, along patterns familiar in postwar eastern Europe, might then proceed.

For a while this hope seemed to have some color of plausibility. One of the nation's leading political personalities, Themistocles Sofoulis, leader of the Liberal party, and a long-time associate of the great Venizelos, stood in opposition to the government. He argued that a policy of conciliation and political moderation would bring the guerrilla bands from the hills, and implied that he and he alone was the man who could carry out such a policy successfully. Certainly the Communists tried to win Sofoulis' confidence. They hoped, in all probability, to see the demoralization of the existing government and the steady worsening of conditions bring about a situation in which Sofoulis would indeed be called to power, and would then be compelled to assign a few of the key ministries to Communist leaders, knowing that without their cooperation he would be unable to make good his promises and persuade the guerrillas to lay down their arms.

Sofoulis, however, had not grown old in Greek politics for nothing, and knew as well as the Communists did that if once they got hold of the Ministries of Interior and War, their power would soon be fastened on the country, and other parties and politicians would speedily be eliminated, including Sofoulis himself. Early in July, therefore, negotiations between Sofoulis and the Communists were broken off, and Sofoulis came out publicly with a denunciation of both the Greek Communist party and the government. [1] Upon meeting this check, Communist policy hardened for war. Previously, the guerrillas had been held more or less in reserve, as a counter in the game of high politics. The Communists had used them to discredit and demoralize the government, and as a lever for bargaining with So-

1. Sofoulis did not long remain in the political wilderness, for he became prime minister on September 7, 1947, and continued to preside over a coalition cabinet until his death in June 1949, when victory in the guerrilla war was already clearly in sight.

foulis. It was only after the first week of July 1947, when the Communist high command was compelled to abandon hope of coming to power legally, that the guerrillas became an instrument of out-and-out civil war.

The consequences of the change in Communist policy soon became manifest. Silently and secretly top Communist leaders left the cities and joined the guerrillas. On July 12, Nicholas Zachariades, the Secretary General of the Greek Communist party, announced through the Communist newspapers (which continued to publish freely until October 18) that the party would establish "free areas" in Greece. Within a couple of days guerrilla forces made large-scale attacks on several towns in northern Greece. None was captured, but the government began to report regular battles in the north, and in Athens and other big towns the police arrested large numbers of known or suspected Communists.

It was just at this time, on July 14, 1947, when full-scale battle had first been joined, that Dwight P. Griswold, who had been appointed to head the American aid mission to Greece, reached Athens. The first shiploads of American supplies followed him a few weeks later.

The turn of events in Greece made the original American aid plan obsolete before it even started to come into operation. As first conceived, the larger share of the $300 million which Congress had allotted to Greece was to be used for economic rehabilitation, while military support was to take second place. Such a distribution of resources scarcely made sense when the scale of military operations was mounting day by day, and when the army was proving itself unable to do more than hold key towns against guerrilla assault. There was no use trying to build power plants in remote places when roads were mined and travel without a large military convoy was unsafe; nor was there much sense in telling the peasants how to improve their farming when they were afraid to go to their fields. The Communists had chosen war, and willy-nilly the American mission found itself compelled to wage war also. The first phase of American aid in Greece, from 1947 to 1949, was therefore a period in which military considerations and programs came first. Everything else had to wait.

The Military Phase of American Aid

For almost an entire year, from July 1947 until June 1948, the offensive remained with the guerrillas. To be sure, the army launched a number of attacks, often accompanied by considerable fanfare in the press; and, as always in guerrilla war, the regular army was able to penetrate and win temporary control of almost any area it desired. But while the army announced empty victories, the number, morale and equipment of the guerrillas steadily increased. Areas which had seen no guerrilla bands in the earliest phases of the war suddenly became infested by them. In February 1948, a band appeared on Mount Parnes, within twenty miles of Athens itself; in the same month a raid was made on the outskirts of Salonika, the second city of Greece. Bands appeared far south in the Peloponnese, until only the islands remained immune from guerrilla activity.

There is no great mystery as to how guerrilla bands were recruited. When two or three organizers came to a new district, and invited the boys of the poor hill villages to take up arms, they regularly found twenty or thirty young fellows — below legal draft age and therefore staying idly and discontentedly at home — who were willing to follow them. With such a core, it was possible to conscript others. Men who were not ready to volunteer, when faced by the alternative of joining up or suffering violent retaliation or even death, found it safest to serve in the guerrilla ranks. The army filled its ranks by conscription only slightly better organized, so that accident often determined on which side a particular individual fought. Desertion from one force to the other occurred quite frequently, especially in the early months of the war.

Much more mystery surrounds the question of how the guerrilla forces secured arms and ammunition. Some certainly came from across the Albanian, Yugoslav and Bulgarian borders, on muleback or carried by conscript peasant women. Probably for this reason, the main center of guerrilla strength always remained along the borders, especially in the wild mountain country adjacent to Albania where the absence of roads hindered the movements of the national army. But more distant parts of Greece, where guerrillas also operated, can scarcely have been supplied by a chain of animal and human pack trains. Small ships, loaded in Albania, certainly brought some supplies to guerrillas of the Peloponnese, and perhaps to other coastal areas. In the early stages of the war, the bands were able to pick up considerable quantities of arms by overrunning isolated police or army posts, and their initial armament came partly from caches in which the wartime ELAS had hidden some of its weapons. Nevertheless, the size and efficiency of the guerrilla armament often surprised the national army, and the organization which permitted the Communists to supply the bands constituted a really remarkable achievement, since they never held any considerable road system and had to move their supplies through rough mountainous country.

It was a considerable time before the army leaders or their new American advisers fully realized the extent and power of the guerrilla movement. At first, the Americans simply decided to deliver supplies for the army as first scheduled, and postpone the program for economic rehabilitation for a few months, until the guerrilla problem had been cleared up. But instead of clearing up, the bands became more numerous. Not until January

1948 did the American mission announce that funds originally scheduled for rehabilitation would be assigned for military needs, in order to increase the size of the national army to 200,000 men. This was, however, a bit disingenuous, since funds classified as "economic" had already been used for constructing emergency military communications, especially roads.

The main form of economic aid, however, was relief for refugees who swarmed in from the countryside, seeking a more secure life in towns. By October 1947 the Greek government announced that 300,000 refugees were dependent on such relief; and at the height of the war their number swelled to 700,000, nearly one tenth of the entire population of the country. Providing even the rudiments of shelter, and the necessary minimum of food and clothing, to such a large number of people constituted the main burden upon American economic aid between 1947 and 1949.

Actually many refugees left their villages and farms unwillingly, compelled to do so by the army. To clear out the population from all of the hill villages that lay within reach became a fixed military policy. The object was to deprive the guerrilla bands of an important source of support. Since the guerrillas had to live off the country, finding food by taking it from the peasants, the army hoped to starve the guerrillas out by removing those peasants who lived in regions where the bands were operating. Yet, carried to its logical completion, such a policy was suicidal, since Greece could not afford to import food for everyone. In general, therefore, the army did not disturb plains villages, where guerrilla raids were no more than hit-and-run affairs. Clearances were confined, for the most part, to villages in the hills, where the guerrillas were close at hand and frequent visitors.

The American military mission, headed by General James Van Fleet, set out vigorously to improve the equipment and training of the national army. This was mainly a matter of money and time. In 1947, there were places and occasions when the guerrillas proved to have better arms than the army possessed. The army's weapons had come from British stocks, left over after the end of World War II, whereas the guerrillas had at least a few more modern weapons — for example a powerful long-range mortar of Russian design — which were superior to comparable British models. By 1948, this was scarcely the case any longer, for the army had by then received a complement of the best and most modern weapons known to the United States. By 1949, the army's superiority was crushing.

Yet equipment and training were not the real problem. The national army was always far superior in numbers to the enemy forces, and any occasional technical inferiority of armament was more than compensated for by the larger numbers of weapons the army possessed. What really mattered was morale. The conscripts of the army mirrored, more or less faithfully, the general political and emotional attitudes of their countrymen. They had little use for the Communists perhaps, but then they had little use for politicians of any stripe, and felt no compelling loyalty to the status quo. To fight fellow Greeks, many of whom were conscripts like themselves, seemed folly; and the efforts of official propaganda to paint the guerrillas as foreign agents met with only limited success.

For the first year of the war, it seems safe to say that the advantage in morale lay with the guerrillas. They had a dream for the future to keep them warm on the mountain tops, even when blankets were short; and the drift of the war certainly seemed to be generally in their favor. Their opponents had no equally effective rallying cry. To fight and die for things as they were could appeal to no one, and to risk one's life to guard against an abstraction called "Communism" could not stir up much enthusiasm in the hearts of the rank and file.

The real turning point of the war came on June 28, 1948, when the Cominform first publicly denounced Tito for deviation from the correct path to socialism. It was, however, some time before the consequences of this event were fully felt in Greece; and not until the campaigns of 1949 did the scales tip definitely against the guerrillas.

The quarrel between Tito and the Cominform presented the leaders of the Greek Communist party with a very awkward choice. They received vital supplies through Yugoslavia, and Yugoslav territory had often provided refuge for a hard-pressed band in time of need. Yet they were also dependent on the good will of Stalin, since their weapons and ammunition, for the most part, originated in territory controlled by the Soviet dictator. For as long as possible, the Greek Communists attempted to escape final and irrevocable choice between the two. After some months, however, they declared in favor of the Cominform, but did so only ambiguously. Even after this decision had become clear, Tito did not at once close his borders to the Greek guerrillas, but the stream of supplies coming through Yugoslavia dwindled and eventually stopped. By the spring of 1949, Albania remained the only important base from which the vital arms and ammunition could come. The Bulgarian frontier was too far away from the tangled mountains where guerrilla strength was concentrated to be of more than minor significance.

When Tito finally closed his borders to the guerrillas in 1949, the military task of the army was much simplified. The Albanian frontier was comparatively short; if it could be sealed off, guerrilla supply lines would be cut. Victory would then be assured as one after another of the guerrilla bands ran out of ammunition. To seal the Albanian border consequently became the army's primary strategic aim in 1949.

Before the army was able to take advantage of its new stra-
tegical position, however, guerrilla morale cracked, so that the
last stages of the fighting did not involve long and hard battles
such as those fought in 1948. At the same time, the morale of
the army stiffened, making it possible for the first time to use to
full effect the superiority in men and matériel which the army
had always enjoyed.

Both changes resulted from a shift in Cominform policy with
respect to the future of Macedonia. Presumably, when Tito was
blacklisted by the authorities of the Cominform, Bulgarian influence in Cominform councils in matters relating to the Balkans
increased. It had been an old ambition of the Bulgarians to create an independent Macedonia, from territories which had
fallen to Greece and Serbia after the second Balkan war of 1913
— a step which for many patriotic Bulgarians was only a halfway house toward incorporation of Macedonia into Bulgaria.
Macedonian national sentiment had achieved enough reality
during the first decades of this century to make it seem possible
to revive its embers in 1949, thus seriously embarrassing Tito,
who was ruling most of the territory inhabited by Macedonian
Slavs.

With this end in view, therefore, the Cominform early in
1949 declared for the establishment of an independent Macedonia within a Balkan federation. The Greek Communist party
had to accept the new line. [2] On March 1, 1949, the "Free

2. Or rather this reassertion of an old Communist nostrum for the Balkans. A Balkan federation, in which Macedonia would constitute one of
the units, had been a central item in the programs of Marxist parties even
before the first world war, and the theme was resumed by Balkan Communist parties and by the Comintern between the wars. The idea was,
however, always peculiarly dear to the Bulgarians, whose influence in the
Comintern in the 1920's and 1930's was much greater than that of any
other Balkan Communist party.

Greece Radio," a Communist mouthpiece located in Rumania, broadcast, with tacit approval, the Cominform resolution in favor of Macedonian independence.

Any Greek who heard such words knew very well that an independent Macedonia could only mean the loss of important Greek territories. Here was an issue for which Greek soldiers were ready and willing to fight. If Communist victory meant the loss of Macedonia (and presumably of Thrace as well), then Communist victory must not come. The effect within the guerrilla forces was no less drastic. The rank and file of the guerrilla bands were patriotic Greeks, too, and most of them sincerely believed that they had been fighting for the best interests of the nation. Nothing their leaders could say would make them willing to give up Macedonia to a Balkan federation, and equivocal efforts of Zachariades and others to explain the issue away could not overcome the new distrust of ultimate Communist intentions in Macedonia. Indeed, even in the inner circle of the Greek Communist party, the new line stirred up bitter controversy. The latent differences between "home grown" and "Russian" Communists flared into angry strife, for only the most thoroughgoing Stalinist was prepared to sacrifice the national interests of Greece on the altar of international Communism and Balkan federation. Markos Vafiades, who had acted as commander in chief of the guerrilla forces from very early days, was among those who would not accept the new policy. Accordingly some weeks before public announcement of the Cominform resolution was made, he was removed from his office for "reasons of health."

In the course of the summer and fall of 1949, the new state of morale showed itself very clearly in the field. Quite apart from their increasing supply problems, guerrilla units were dispirited and no longer fought very hard, while the new dash and energy of the national army won the admiration of many American army officers who were "advising" its formations. In effect, the final stages of the army's attack became almost a victory parade. Early in September 1949, what survived of the main guerrilla force in the north broke through a slender army cordon and retreated into Albania. On October 16 the "Free Greece Radio" announced that military operations had been suspended, although at the same time it declared that the Greek guerrilla units would not be disbanded. In spite of this last threat, the war was over. The national army had won; the Greek government was once more secure within its frontiers.

Victory had been very costly. The American financial contribution was substantial, totaling more than four times the sum President Truman had originally asked Congress to appropriate for Greece. Appendix 1 gives an idea of the scale of American operations.

Yet these sums represented only a small fraction of the real cost of the fighting. There is no possible way of calculating how many persons were killed, since neither side kept accurate records, and civilian casualties were not counted at all. Nor is there much use in trying to create statistics relating to material damage to houses, communications, livestock and the like. It seems quite certain, however, that these losses more than equaled the reconstruction which had been accomplished between 1944 and 1947. The country as a whole was worse off in 1949 than it had been in 1944 and 1945, when the severe losses of the occupation years were still fresh.

Clearly, the task of reconstruction and construction was going to be much larger than United States officials had estimated in 1947. Except for main roads and ports, which had been rebuilt and improved during the course of the fighting, almost everything planned in 1947 still remained to be done in 1949. On top of this, the fresh damages of the guerrilla war had to be made good if Greece were to arrive at a satisfactory and more or less self-sustaining economic level.

In one sense, nevertheless, the drastic upheaval of the guerrilla war may have helped the future rehabilitation of the country. The age-old conservatism of the villages had been shaken, as never before, and resistance to innovation for the future was correspondingly weakened. Peasant boys who had spent two or three years in the army, been trained in the use of various types of military machinery, traveled to and fro in Greece and met men from all parts of the country could never be quite the same again when they returned home. For that matter, few of their homes had been unaffected by the war. This was especially true among the 700,000 refugees. These people had spent anything up to two and a half years in or near the larger towns and cities, living mostly in idleness. Old routines and habits were naturally disturbed by such a change; in particular, the women, who in normal times would have stayed very close to home and an immemorial routine of life, saw a different world. Urban horizons created new attitudes and expectations among the refugees, and alienated them from traditional peasant values more drastically than ever before. The short-term consequence was increased discontent with their lot in life; yet one may argue that in the longer run an adjustment of rural customs and expectations to urbanized standards of life may facilitate the eventual stabilization of the economy — above all by impelling the peasants to restrict the number of children born into rural poverty.

Yet this gain, if gain it was, could scarcely be detected in 1949. Instead, restless discontent among the refugees was all too evident. Many families had no desire to return to the hard life of the hills, all the more since most of their houses had been destroyed or severely damaged, their livestock had been scattered and killed, and their tools lost or sold. The thoroughness with which these people's lives had been uprooted and the drastic material losses they had suffered made them a particularly unstable and dissatisfied element, seeking not so much the old familiar life as something new. To find means to resettle these refugees and start them back to productive occupations was, in fact, the first and most urgent problem of the postwar period.

The Period of Rehabilitation

When Congress agreed to President Truman's proposal for special aid to Greece and Turkey, and assigned $300 million to Greece, the grant was for one year only. Long before the twelve months were up, it became quite obvious that American aid would have to be prolonged, since the guerrilla war showed no sign of coming to an end. Meanwhile, American policy had taken a further step. In June 1947, Secretary of State George C. Marshall had offered American aid to all of Europe, and after long negotiation a four-year plan was evolved for the economic rehabilitation of those countries which accepted the proposal. Greece was among the countries that came into the Marshall plan. Consequently from April 1948 onward, American economic aid programs in Greece became a part of an over-all European recovery administration. This put American planning in Greece on a four-year basis, with 1952 as the target date by which economic and social stability should be achieved.

The prolongation of the guerrilla war until the fall of 1949 made this target date increasingly unrealistic as the months of war went by. Little could be done toward the long-term development of the country until peace and security had returned to the countryside. Relief for refugees and indigents, together with construction projects directly serving military purposes, absorbed nearly all available funds. Therefore, when victory at last came definitely within sight, American planners embarked upon a "crash" program, attempting to crowd four years' economic development into the two and a half years that remained. To make such a program possible, American authorities in Athens and Washington were prepared to continue and even to increase the high level of appropriations which had been necessary during the war period. For example, in 1950–51, a total of $435.1 million was assigned to Greece, of which $284.4 million was earmarked for economic and $150.7 million for military aid (Appendix 1). This was the largest sum appropriated in any single fiscal year during the entire American aid program in Greece.

If success was to be achieved, and Greece made self-supporting in so short a time, it was clear that drastic steps were called for. In general, the American program envisioned heavy investment in communications, industry and agriculture by the Greek government, and called for a radical economy in other types of government expenditure (including military expenditure) in order to reduce inflation and make local funds available to pay the internal costs of the investment program. More specifically, the Americans set out to reduce the relief rolls which had taken such a large proportion of aid funds in the war years; to restore communications; to expand industrial and agricultural production; and to reform the Greek government. Like Hercules of old, the American mission boldly undertook all these difficult enterprises, intending to sweep the Augean stables clean and erect a gleaming palace upon the battered structure of the Greek economy in no more than two and a half years. John Nuveen, a vigorous and outspoken businessman, replaced Dwight Griswold as head of the mission, but his relationship to the United

States Ambassador was left unclear, and when the two men clashed, quarrels within the American official community in Greece still further complicated the tasks which the mission had assumed.

The most urgent problem, for both financial and social reasons, was to get the refugees back home to their villages and off the relief rolls. As a general rule, everyone was required to return to his former home, whether or not he wished to do so. One may question the wisdom of repopulating some of the hill villages, where local resources were totally inadequate to support the number of people who had lived there before. In 1950, however, the choice was between sending the refugees back and continuing a prohibitively expensive relief program indefinitely. No less than $50 million, or 22 per cent of all government expenditures, had been consigned to relief in the last year of the war.

The returning refugees were given considerable help in reestablishing themselves. Relief payments were continued for a time after their return to their villages, often in the form of work relief programs which provided pay for labor on village improvements — construction of schools, churches, water supply systems, roads and the like. Grants of materials and of money helped with the repair or rebuilding of houses, and the government also provided some livestock and tools free of charge.

By June 1950 almost all the refugees had returned to their villages, and a year later nearly all of the special aid programs designed to help them get back on their feet had come to an end. The hill villages of Greece had been repopulated and at least partially rebuilt, sometimes with much improved amenities. Yet the fundamental problem of how these people could make a living on the barren hillsides was not solved; and it could not be solved short of a large-scale urban and industrial development of the country, for which there was not time. Back in their hills, the returned refugees at least could produce something; in the towns they would simply have added to the ranks of the unemployed, and their discontent, being massed into a few large centers, could more easily have come to political expression. This was perhaps enough to justify the sometimes highhanded methods required to send them back to their former homes.

The real justification, however, must be the use made of funds released from direct relief by the resettlement program. Insofar as these were used for productive economic investment, contributing to the future wealth of the country and opening new employment opportunities for the superabundant population, it can be argued that the greater good of the greater number was served.

Before either industry or agriculture could be expected to flourish it was necessary to restore and improve the transportation system of the country. A good start in this direction had been made during the fighting, since the main roads and ports had been required for military movement. But there remained many parts of the country where mule tracks provided the only means of access. It was not a coincidence that many of the refugees of the guerrilla war period lived in such places; and when they were sent back to their former homes, an extensive program of road building was started, using refugee labor to open simple dirt roads connecting their villages with the main highways.

This was partly work relief, partly also a matter of social and even of military policy, since it seemed unsafe, in view of the great success the guerrillas had had in roadless country, to leave a substantial portion of the population of the nation in places where wheeled vehicles could not penetrate. With roads, these villages might find their place in the general economic nexus of Greek society, and come for the first time under the full vigor of government administration. Too much of the old style of economic self-sufficiency and communal isolation might facilitate some future guerrilla movement; and without easier communication with the outside world, any possibilities of economic development that existed in the hills would be cut off from the start.

For these reasons, therefore, the building of third-class unpaved roads was pressed ahead vigorously. By 1951, 4,437 kilometers of such roads were in use. This was more than 2.4 times the length of the prewar network of equivalent roads. [3] During the same years several thousand trucks and buses were imported, so that it became easy, as never before, for people and goods to travel to and from the urban centers of the land into its far corners. After a lull, road-building programs were resumed in 1953; and as the road network expanded, a really radical change came to older geographical and social relations.

In fact, the construction of second- and third-class roads, together with substantial improvement of the trunk roads, can be said to constitute the most fundamental of all the great changes wrought by the American aid program in Greece. This was especially true if one considers social and psychological as well as economic consequences. For with the breakdown of traditional village isolation, which the daily arrival of a bus implied, urban attitudes and an orientation toward market farming began to penetrate regions formerly set apart by the primitive nature of the transportation system. It will be many years before the full consequences work themselves out, but no observer could doubt that by 1956 profound changes in peasant life and attitudes al-

3. National Statistical Services of Greece, *Statistical Yearbook of Greece, 1955*, Athens, 1956, Table 155.

ready were under way, changes which were largely fed and maintained by the new ease of travel and transport. [4]

Once the road system had reached a more or less satisfactory condition, the next big job was to restore the railroads. This required rather heavy expenditure because of the mountainous nature of the terrain and the thoroughness with which the Germans had destroyed bridges and rolling stock upon their retreat in 1944. Only a small part of the rail system had been restored before the guerrilla war once more brought fresh damages. Nevertheless, the problem was a straightforward one of bringing in the necessary material and equipment; and in less than two years the entire rail system was back in operation.

By 1951 the basic transport system of the country was not only restored to its prewar level, but was in much better shape than ever before. In the years that followed, emphasis was put on telecommunications and the improvement of minor ports for the use of coastal shipping. These involved more modest expenditure than had gone into roads and railroads in the first years.

Government investment in roads and railroads was a matter of course, so that American officials had no difficulty in transferring funds for these purposes directly to the Greek authorities who spent the money and supervised the work. As far as industry was concerned, however, the fact that private ownership and management was traditional, and that neither the Americans nor the Greeks wished to change this state of affairs, introduced a complication into the administration of the aid program. Everyone wished to see a vigorous program of indus-

4. After 1949, the United States Information Service in Greece embarked upon a program of distributing a radio to every village. As a result, the impact of the Athens radio station upon the back country increased tremendously, and came to supplement the effects of easier transport in urbanizing village outlooks.

trial investment, but there was no prospect that private capital could be found to carry it through. If new factories were to be built and old ones modernized, it was clear that a channel would have to be found through which funds might pass from the United States government to the hands of private Greek entrepreneurs. Accordingly, a Central Loan Committee was set up with the duty of making loans to deserving private companies with capital provided from American sources. Both Greeks and Americans sat on this committee.

Granting and withholding such loans obviously offered a splendid opportunity for Greek officials and politicians to play favorites, and they sometimes did. Sometimes, also, industrialists withdrew, or attempted to withdraw, a part of their own capital from their factories when loans were made to them. The reason for this was that industrial investment was not very attractive. Capitalists could often find safer or more profitable uses for their money, where it would be less subject to governmental control and taxation. A more serious defect of the industrial loan program was that no very great effort was made to enforce repayment. Many businesses found it convenient to default, since the steady inflation of the currency meant that if repayment could be put off for a few years, only some fraction of the original value of the loan would have to be repaid. As a result, default became widespread, indeed usual, and the Loan Committee could not reinvest much of its original capital through fresh loans, as had been intended. Hence the loan program bogged down after the first year or two, and fell a good deal short of what the Americans had hoped for. [5]

Nevertheless, government loans to private industry, together with the improvements in transport and the general amelioration of conditions which the end of active fighting entailed, sufficed to raise the output of industry above prewar levels. Ac-

5. Cf. Appendix 5.

cording to the index figures compiled by the Greek Federation
of Industries, industrial production in 1950 was 110 per cent of
the 1939 figure, having risen from 67 per cent in 1947. This
rapid recovery reflected the fact that the nation's industrial
plant, being concentrated in large cities for the most part and
especially in Athens-Piraeus, had not suffered very widespread
physical damage during the war years. A few relatively minor
repairs, above all a supply of spare parts for worn machinery,
together with loans of working capital, sufficed to put most factories back into full-scale operation; and since some factories
had not been working to their full capacity in 1939, it was not
so very difficult to surpass the prewar figures. Mining was very
different. Most mines, being in exposed places, had been very
thoroughly looted of their machinery during the war, so that
far more extensive investment was required before operations
could be resumed. As a result, by 1950 the index figure for mining stood at only 21 per cent of 1939. [6]

To get the old plants back in operation again was certainly an
important achievement. It did not, however, do anything to
solve the chronic financial and marketing problems which stood
in the way of long-range industrial advance. Until 1953, domestic industry operated with almost complete protection from
foreign competition. Imports of all sorts were licensed by the
government in order to conserve foreign exchange; and since
there was a serious shortage of foreign currencies to pay for
vital imports, it made sense to refuse licenses for the import of
anything that could be produced within the country, no matter
how expensive the home product might be. Hence, manufac-
turers did not have to worry about world price levels. In many
branches of industry there was no internal competition either,
since a single factory or firm dominated or even completely
monopolized the production of a given type of goods.

6. *Statistical Yearbook of Greece, 1955,* Table 122.

Under such circumstances, it is not strange that prices were set high. Naturally, the potential domestic market was thereby restricted, not to speak of the impossibility of competing in the export field with more developed and more favorably situated countries. Yet the desire of Greek industrialists to gain a high percentage of profit on a restricted volume of goods was only in part responsible for this situation. Industry also confronted real physical disadvantages. Power was expensive, since it derived from imported fuels; and a very large proportion of industrial raw materials had to be brought into the country from abroad. Consequently, even a well-managed and technically efficient factory would find it hard to produce at prices competitive in the world market; and few of the factories were well managed. To pad expenses was often the best way to reduce taxation; and many an owner found it convenient to take his profits and to reward his senior employees by authorizing himself and them to draw up lush or fraudulent expense accounts.

Partly because of these difficulties, and partly because improvement of agriculture promised quicker and larger returns, American aid programs in the years just after the guerrilla war emphasized agriculture more than industry. In 1950 a new agricultural extension service was organized. Great efforts were made to recruit and train men who would be able to win the confidence of the peasants, and who would not shrink, as prewar agricultural agents had often done, from getting their hands dirty in the fields when practical demonstration of some new technique was in order. In time this effort turned out to be very successful. By 1956, agricultural extension agents had become a real influence in the countryside, and many villages had profited handsomely from their advice, receiving help from their hands as well.

In the short run, however, the recovery and expansion of agricultural production was more dramatically assisted by making fertilizer available to the farmers at prices they could afford. This by itself in case after case increased yields as much as 100 per cent, since before and during the war many farmers had not used fertilizer at all, partly from ignorance, and partly because its price was high and the danger of incurring a debt which they could not repay frightened them. Figures of the Ministry of Agriculture on fertilizer consumption suggest the scale of this simple, but highly effective, change: 19,590 metric tons were consumed in 1946–47, 54,887 in 1950–51, 79,968 in 1955–56.

In addition to the expanded use of fertilizers, agriculture benefited from the introduction of new crops and improved types of seed, from artificial insemination of cattle and sheep designed to raise the quality of the livestock, and from the repair, improvement and extension of water control and irrigation works. These measures all took time to bring large-scale results, but their effectiveness in increasing the food supply of the country and building up an exportable surplus was never in doubt.

The most dramatic success of this sort was the introduction of rice growing in a number of swampy coastal areas which had previously lain waste, or were used only as seasonal rough pasture land. An average of only 4,000 metric tons of rice had been grown before the war; this was increased to 56,000 tons by 1951, and by 1954 the figure had gone up to 86,000 tons. Not only was enough produced to supply the normal consumption of the country, but a small quantity became available for export. Moreover, the laborious work of cultivating the rice provided much needed seasonal employment for several thousand peasant families in the neighborhood of the new fields.

No general index of agricultural production was attempted until 1950, and even then the arbitrary character of crop estimates in a country where much was consumed directly by the producers probably made the figure quite unreliable. It was estimated, however, that by 1950 crop production was somewhat above the prewar level, with the exception of tobacco, which stood slightly below the 1935–38 average. Livestock production, on the other hand, lagged far behind, owing to the extensive destruction of herds during the war years.

The social and psychological difficulties that stood in the way of rapid industrial development had an analogue among the peasants in their age-old conservatism and attachment to familiar ways of doing things. But the war with all its attendant disturbances of familiar routine had already done much to break this resistance down; and when tangible advantage was demonstrated, the peasants did not hang back for long before adopting new methods, crops, seeds and the like. Successful industrialism required far more complex social and psychological, financial and technical adjustment — adjustments which could scarcely be made in a short period of time; agricultural advance required only practical demonstration of what could be done, whereupon the shrewdness and energy of the peasant family could be depended upon to put into effect what they knew would benefit them personally and directly.

Problems of food marketing, processing, grading and so on partook more of the complexities of industrial organization, and here the efforts of the American mission and of Greek officials were less successful. However, the restoration of the transport system much facilitated marketing. In particular, improved roads allowed the Athens market to extend tentacles far up-country, even for fruit and other perishable crops.

Part of the theory behind the emphasis upon agricultural development was that an improved agriculture could help remedy the drastic disbalance in international payments which the country had inherited from the war. [7] Throughout modern times Greece had depended upon agricultural products to pay

7. See Appendices 2 and 3.

for manufactures and other imports. The climate and traditional peasant skills provided the country with a number of high-value agricultural exports: tobacco, currants, olive oil and a few others. Of these, tobacco was by far the most important, since Greek tobacco was of a special quality, used for blending in American cigarettes and attractive also to German taste. Sale of tobacco constituted the largest single item in the foreign trade balance. This had been so ever since the tobacco regions of Thrace and Macedonia were brought within Greek frontiers in 1912–13.

To restore and enlarge agricultural exports, therefore, was clearly the most promising way to attack the desperate problem of the balance of payments. Until the country came somewhere near balancing imports with exports, there could be no prospect of financial or economic stability, and this, after all, was the overriding aim of the entire American aid program.

During the war and postwar years, the problem had been worsened by the fact that Greece ceased to produce enough food to feed her population. In 1948–49, for example, when the refugee relief program was at its height, imports of food totaled $167 million, and agricultural exports amounted to only $83.7 million. By 1950–51, food imports had been reduced to $112.2 million; agricultural exports had, however, scarcely increased, totaling only $84 million. [8] In other words, increases in agricultural production were mainly consumed within the country, while exports were hindered by a variety of marketing problems, pre-eminently by the fact that the internal price level tended to make potential exports too expensive. As a matter of fact, large quantities of tobacco remained in warehouses be-

8. By 1953–54, when favorable weather brought unusually good crops, the ratio was reversed, with only $40.2 million of food imports and $111 million in exports of agricultural products. U. S. Operations Mission/ Greece, *The American Aid Programs in Greece*, Athens, 1954, p. 12.

cause purchasers could not be found at the prices set by the government. (Tobacco and wheat were the only crops marketed under a system of government price supports.)

One temporary solution to this problem was devaluation of the currency. For psychological reasons, however, government authorities were reluctant to change the official value of the drachma as against foreign currencies, since such an act was bound to stir memories of past inflations among the people and reinforce their already lively distrust of the national currency. Nevertheless, in June 1951 the drachma was devalued, its official rate being set at 15,000 to the dollar instead of 5,000 as before. This served, temporarily, to bring Greek export prices into line with general world prices, and helped clear the tobacco warehouses.

The fundamental problem, of course, was to find means by which to check the running inflation which had characterized the nation's finances since the war years. The main factor behind the chronic inflation was the spendthrift habits of the government. Expenditures had been met only partly by taxation. Note issue and the consignment of "counterpart funds" [9] to the general budget of the government had been necessary to make up the balance. From the American point of view, the use of counterpart funds to pay the running expenses of the government was intolerable. Instead of being used for investment that might contribute to the expansion of the economy, the money was going down the drain, supporting a host of pensioners, civil servants and soldiers. In 1949–50, for example, when this use of counterpart funds reached its peak, no less than 1,516 mil-

9. "Counterpart funds" were drachmae that accrued to the government through sale of goods imported under American aid programs. Such sums were placed in a special account in the Bank of Greece, and the American aid mission retained special jurisdiction over the use to which they might be put.

lion drachmae (41.6 per cent of all the counterpart funds that accrued to the government's account in that year) went for budget balancing. By comparison, the entire cost of the refugee housing and rehabilitation program amounted to only 1,214 million drachmae. [10]

Fiscal reorganization therefore seemed imperative, if solid progress toward economic stabilization were to be achieved. A program of tax reform and more rigorous collection of taxes already on the books was only part of what, in the view of American officials, needed to be done. Somehow the government budget must be brought into balance, and this required rigorous pruning of the superabundant personnel of the civil service, reduction of the army, and parsimony in all other expenditures. In addition, the Americans were firmly convinced that decentralization of authority would simplify and speed up government action, and they believed also that a reduction in the number of central ministries and a clearer definition of their respective spheres of responsibility would bring cheaper and better government.

It was not difficult to get Greek politicians to agree that governmental administration needed to be reformed, and they were quite willing to pay lip service to the principle of a balanced budget. But when it came to action they were anything but enthusiastic. Every one of the American proposals for governmental reform threatened some group or other with loss of livelihood or of power, and the gain that might come in time would benefit the nation as a whole rather than any single and well-defined group. It is in the nature of democratic politics (and perhaps of all politics) that reforms of such a character are very hard to push through. They certainly proved so in Greece.

While the American authorities set to work in the spirit of the "crash" program, with 1952 as the target date for the com-

10. U. S. Operations Mission/Greece, *Statistical Data Book,* Table 45.

pletion of economic rehabilitation, Greek politicians found no
real need to do more than agree in words with American demands for economy and reorganization in government. So long
as the Americans were prepared to pump hundreds of millions
of dollars into the economy each year, why should the Greek
government not run an unbalanced budget and let the balance
of foreign payments take care of itself? The Americans would
have to make the deficits good; and if they complained of the
use to which their funds were put, one could mollify them with
promises for the future. Greeks were very much inclined to
feel that the United States owed them a great debt of gratitude
for having fought the guerrilla war and stopped the advance of
Communism; and shortcomings could always be blamed on the
tremendous and very real losses the country had suffered from
the prolonged fighting it had seen. Some politicians were even
inclined to feel that it would not really be a good thing to balance the budget and correct the shortfall in exports, for if these
things were done, then the crying need for American aid would
disappear, and the country might then be left to fend for itself economically.

Needless to say, such attitudes seemed utterly irresponsible
to the Americans, but how to combat them was difficult to decide. The Americans had come to Greece to support democracy,
and to defend the right of the people to choose their government freely — or so it had often been said. But the sort of government that emerged from the electoral process in Greece was
one that the Americans found very hard to take. In this di-
lemma, democratic theory soon gave way before the practical
pressure to get things done. In 1950, therefore, the Americans
embarked upon a determined and distinctly highhanded effort
to get a government that would more nearly suit their wishes.

The first maneuver on the part of United States Ambassador Henry F. Grady, who took the lead in this matter, was to

call for fresh elections almost as soon as the guerrilla war was over. He had the Greek constitution on his side, since the parliament, which had been elected in 1946, was nearing its legal term. Counter arguments, that the country was not yet sufficiently pacified and the electoral lists not properly drawn, were brushed aside, and elections duly took place in March 1950. What the Americans had hoped was that a fairly cohesive group of center parties would win a majority in parliament, proceed to organize a strong and stable government, and then seriously undertake the program of reform, reorganization, economy and investment which the Americans had prepared. Their hopes were not realized. No clear majority resulted, and the first prime minister who succeeded in forming a cabinet on the basis of the new parliament was Sophocles Venizelos, a man definitely *persona non grata* to the Americans.

Trying to make the best of a bad business, therefore, Ambassador Grady intervened again by writing a letter to the new prime minister in which the full reform program was set forth, with the additional statement that since his cabinet did not seem to have the necessary strength to carry through such a program, cuts in American aid might be necessary. This letter was made public before Venizelos had an opportunity to reply to it. The displeasure of the Americans had been made perfectly clear, and after a few days, Venizelos resigned. A new prime minister, Nicholas Plastiras, took over with the blessing of the Americans.

Yet, from the American point of view, Plastiras and his cabinet did not turn out to be very satisfactory instruments, either. Programs for reform were agreed to, with some show of determination, but action did not follow. Many of Plastiras' supporters were lukewarm, and his cabinet did not command firm support in the Chamber of Deputies. No American pressure for governmental economy could compel reluctant deputies to vote laws that they disliked, or to support a government that really took action against their wishes. As a result, Plastiras was out within six months, and Venizelos came back to office as prime minister. A new American ambassador, John Peurifoy, arrived in Athens, and in September 1950 declared that the United States government was completely neutral in matters of internal Greek politics. This pious falsehood was in effect a public confession of defeat. The Greek government had not been reformed, economy in government expenditure had not been enforced; note issue and the consignment of counterpart funds for the running expenses of the government continued almost as freely as before.

Since intervention on the political level had not worked, United States officials decided that economic pressure might be effective. Accordingly, in September 1950 the American mission announced that aid appropriations would be sharply reduced for the coming fiscal year. The letter in which this decision was announced explained that because the government had not carried through essential fiscal and administrative reforms, it had become evident that effective use could not be made of the amount of aid previously scheduled for 1951–52.

The meaning of this ultimatum was clear. The American aid mission had determined that it would no longer tolerate the use of counterpart funds for balancing the national budget. American money was to be used for productive investment, or it would not be used at all. Venizelos took this second American broadside more or less in stride. He promptly promised to carry through all the reforms which the American mission demanded. But this time he did not leave office. The Americans no longer had a rival candidate they wished to install, and had perhaps come to feel that one Greek politician was very much like another.

Even had Venizelos been completely sincere in his promises — and this was doubtful — he would have found it very hard to live up to them. The weight of effective opposition to the American program was as great as ever, and support for it within the country was almost nonexistent. Plans were made, but progress remained painfully slow.

A new factor in the situation was the Korean war, which broke out in June 1950. This event on the other side of the world had strong repercussions in Greece, for it made one essential element in the original American blueprint for speedy economic stabilization suddenly seem the height of folly. To reduce the armed forces of the country to a level which could be sustained economically now seemed likely to invite attack. But without drastic reduction in Greek military expenditures, the whole American plan for stabilization by 1952 became unworkable.

Obviously, a new look at American aid programs and policies in Greece was now called for. By degrees the hope of setting the country on its feet through radical and speedy action, large-scale investment, wholesale reform and highhanded pressure was abandoned. Greece would not be stabilized by 1952 as once planned; the aid program would have to continue longer; military considerations and strength would once again loom large in American calculations; the whole pace of American efforts in Greece would have to be slowed down.

This did not become evident all at once, but it is clear enough in retrospect that American policy in Greece took a new turn in the fall of 1950. The reduced scale of expenditure did not come into effect until July 1951, when the new fiscal year began, and many elements in the original "crash" program for economic rehabilitation survived in subsequent planning. Nevertheless, the rosy optimism and impatient haste of the first period were gone; but so were the worst legacies of the guerrilla war period. Longer-term economic reconstruction and the maintenance of a satisfactory military posture vis-à-vis Communist satellites in the Balkans became the two major concerns of the revised American aid programs. Efforts toward political and fiscal reform remained on the agenda, but were pressed more discreetly.

The real achievement of the years 1949–50 had been to restore Greek agriculture, communications and industry to something above their prewar levels. If the problems which still remained had not been so overwhelming, this would have seemed a very satisfactory result.

Long-Term Development and Reform

Between 1951 and 1954, American appropriations for economic aid to Greece tapered off fairly rapidly, as the figures in Appendix 1 show. Actual deliveries dropped off more slowly, owing to carry-over from year to year. In 1953–54, for example, when fresh appropriations for economic aid to Greece reached the minimum of $21.3 million, actual deliveries were valued at $59 million; and in 1955–56 the total amount of money available to the Greek government from American sources was $82.7 million, although not all of it was spent, since some portion was in its turn carried over to the following fiscal year. [11]

Since the exact figures for military aid to Greece have been kept secret since 1951–52, it is impossible to be precise as to the total amount of all the various American aid programs. From what has been published, however, it is clear that military aid appropriations dropped less sharply, averaging not quite $100 million a year between 1951 and 1955. [12] If it is assumed that this rate continued in 1955–56 — and there is no reason to think it did not — then the grand total of American aid to Greece during the nine-year period from May 1947 to June 1956 may be

11. U. S. Information Service press release, April 27, 1956; data for 1953–54 from U. S. Operations Mission/Greece, *Statistical Data Book*, Table 42.

12. U. S. Information Service press release, April 27, 1956.

calculated at about $2,565 million. Taking the population of Greece in 1951 as a rough median for the period, this total implies that the United States Congress appropriated about $335 for every man, woman and child in the country during these nine years. No other nation in the world received such intensive assistance from the United States government, nor — in spite of the fact that nearly half the sum went for military purposes — has any other "underdeveloped" country enjoyed so much governmental foreign aid per capita during the postwar period. These facts lend a degree of special significance to the recent history of Greece. Nowhere else have the potentialities and limits of governmental foreign aid been so thoroughly explored.

In 1953 it looked as though the economic side of American aid to Greece was about to taper off to comparatively trivial proportions, and that the Greeks would be left to sink or swim more or less on their own, save always for military assistance from the United States. In 1954–55, however, the allotment of economic aid increased for the first time in four years, and the appropriation was increased again in 1955–56. The increases were accounted for largely by loans and grants made by the United States government to help dispose of surplus farm commodities which were embarrassing the administration at home. In 1955–56, when this new policy had come fully into effect, American economic aid to Greece consisted of a "pipeline" of $16 million, representing unused balances from previous years, $800,000 for technical assistance, a new allotment of $33.7 million, and no less than $33 million in the form of loans and outright grants for the purchase of surplus farm commodities. [13]

To have large quantities of food available cheaply and on generous credit terms was certainly a help to the Greeks. The portion of American surplus commodities which was given

13. *Ibid.*

away freely in the form of school lunches, charitable distribution and the like helped to relieve chronic undernourishment. Still, neither the Greek government nor the American economic mission in Greece would have used funds for such purposes had they been planning from a Greek point of view. Food was needed, but other things were needed more if the economy was to be made self-supporting. This is to say that after 1954 the aid program was reshaped to serve American more distinctly than Greek governmental interests.

Up to 1951, American personnel had taken the main responsibility, in fact if not always in legal form, for the planning and carrying through of reconstruction and rehabilitation. Advisers had been installed in the ministries, field representatives had been stationed all over the country to check up on actual performance, and when things went wrong or failed to conform to American ideas, vigorous efforts were made to alter the situation through "advice" that often took on a peremptory tone. After 1951, as the scale of American aid diminished, advisers were withdrawn one by one, and Greek officials became more and more genuinely in charge of administration, if not always of policy.

American influence on Greek governmental policy remained very great. Direct intervention and day-by-day supervision gave way to indirect, but nonetheless quite effective, fiscal control. What happened was this: In general, the American economic mission put a veto upon the use of American funds for new projects which had not already been started. The mission further required the Greek government to justify the continuation of old projects, before fresh allotments of American funds were made. Adequate justification for all such expenditures called not only for detailed plans and arguments as to the value of any particular undertaking; the Americans also demanded to know how each project would fit into the country's general pattern of economic development. Moreover, plans had to be drawn up in both real and financial terms, so that the Americans could pass judgment upon the fiscal as well as the physical practicability of whatever the Greeks proposed to do with American aid. Thus, even when the amount of such aid shrank to comparatively small proportions, the real control of the American mission over Greek governmental policy remained very broad. The only sort of planning that satisfied the Americans was "global," so that, before the mission would approve the expenditure of any American funds, the general, over-all financial and economic plans of the Greek government had to be made acceptable to them.

American policy in Greece was not, however, perfectly clear or unambiguous. On the one hand, the temper of the United States Congress toward continued appropriations for foreign aid had to be considered; on the other, American experts attempted to weigh the real needs and capacities of the Greek economy. The will of Congress naturally prevailed in any case of conflict, since it was Congress that ultimately controlled the purse strings. Yet officials of the economic mission tended to justify decreases in American aid by pointing to the dangers of inflation within Greece, arguing for a slower rate of investment, a balanced budget and a conservative financial policy; while the Greek ministers and senior civil servants regularly pleaded for more rapid economic expansion and larger appropriations of United States funds, even if their use involved further inflation. How much of the American position in these arguments was dictated by theoretical economic conviction and how much by a desire to find good reasons for trimming Greek requests to a size palatable to Congress would be difficult to say. Both motives were often at work, but insofar as the latter was predominant, it gave a certain ring of unreality to the high theoretical arguments employed by both sides.

A second, and far more important, ambiguity of American policy in Greece arose from the different outlooks of the economic and military missions. [14] After Korea, American policy called for maintenance of a strong Greek army; and after 1951, when Greece was admitted to NATO, military policy in Greece became a part of general NATO planning. The soldiers naturally thought mainly in "real" as opposed to "fiscal" terms, and were but little impressed by theoretical arguments about the dangers of inflation if large numbers of men were employed to build air bases, for example. Hence the words of American economists and the acts of American colonels in Greece often ran at cross purposes. It would have been difficult indeed for the Greeks to please both at the same time, and since the Greek government agreed with the American military that strong defenses were essential to the country, and found the task of balancing the budget inherently distasteful, the budget remained out of balance and inflation continued, though not as rapidly as before.

In 1951, when the American economic mission put a general veto upon the use of American funds for financing new projects in Greece, the policy was conceived as a temporary one. The basic aim of the American aid programs in Greece had not yet

14. After some rather unseemly quarrels between leading American official representatives in the country during the first years of the American aid program in Greece, the economic and military missions were combined in name, but scarcely in fact, as the United States Operations Mission/ Greece, and the heads of each were subordinated to the United States Ambassador.

What I refer to as the "American economic mission" went by a number of different official names: ECA (Economic Cooperation Administration) until 1952; then MSA (Mutual Security Administration) until 1954; then ICA (International Cooperation Administration). But despite changes of name, the reality remained the same, since personnel and policy shifted only slowly and piecemeal. ECA, MSA and ICA may properly be treated as one and the same organization as far as Greece was concerned.

been achieved. The economy was still not self-sustaining, and many ambitious and inherently sound plans which had been painstakingly drawn up had not gone beyond a paper stage. Therefore, somewhat vague hopes were held out to the Greeks that when and if they succeeded in putting their financial affairs in order, increased aid from the United States might be forthcoming once again; and it was hinted that many of the projects which had to be shelved when American aid was reduced might thus come to life once more.

This combination of stick and carrot jarred the Greek government into making serious efforts to increase its income and reduce unproductive expenditure. By 1952–53, for instance, the deficit in the regular national budget was only 337 million "new" drachmae, according to the calculation of the Americans. This deficit was barely more than a fifth of what it had been in 1949–50. In the same year, the deficit in what was called the "investment" budget was 598 million "new" drachmae, as against the high point of 2,100 million in 1950–51. [15]

These figures represented a real effort to increase government income and keep expenditures down. This effort, together with

15. U. S. Operations Missions/Greece, *Statistical Data Book,* Table 125. "New" drachmae were issued in May 1954, at the rate of one new to 1,000 old drachmae.

American calculations have been used here, since it was on this basis that American decisions were made. Greek budgetary figures, published in *Statistical Yearbook of Greece, 1955,* Table 196, are compiled differently, and by counting American aid as income, actually show a budget surplus from 1952 onward (Appendix 4). This was not the way Americans viewed the situation, however, and in 1956 a debate still went on between Greek officials, who proudly pointed to a balanced budget, and American personnel, who pointed with alarm to the continuing "inflationary gap." The matter resolved itself into technical questions of accountancy upon which I cannot pass judgment; but the undoubted fact that currency circulation continued to increase at a rate far higher than any increase in productivity seems evidence enough to prove that the American figures are less misleading than the Greek ones.

important changes in the political climate of the country, persuaded the Americans to relax somewhat the restrictive policy they had adopted in 1951. Accordingly, the economic aid appropriation in 1954–55 increased modestly, even apart from the increases arising from the new program for disposing of American agricultural surpluses which started in the same fiscal year.

Yet even during the lean years, 1951–54, American aid to the Greek economy by no means ceased. Projects which had been started before the crackdown were continued when they could be justified to the Americans and fitted within the appropriations made each year by Congress. By all odds the largest and most significant of these was the construction of four electric power stations and of a high-tension transmission system to link the three largest of the new generators together.

The provision of cheaper power had been a major preoccupation of economic planners for Greece ever since the days of UNRRA. Everyone recognized that what the country needed most was an expansion of productive employment; and industry, if only it could be made to flourish, promised to provide such employment as nothing else could. Everyone further recognized that as long as power was expensive, industry could scarcely be expected to flourish. The obvious answer, therefore, was to harness the potential hydroelectric power of the country to a national electric grid that could feed industry cheaply enough to allow technically efficient factories to compete on world markets. Lignite, of which Greece has at least two large deposits, offered another possible source of cheaper power.

Unfortunately, promising hydroelectric sites were concentrated in the northwest, far from the main population centers, in wild and remote country. While the guerrilla war was in progress, these regions constituted the center of guerrilla strength, and nothing could be done on the spot. Nevertheless, as early as 1948, an American firm was given a contract to prepare engineering plans for the construction of a national power net. Plans were complete by 1950, and after some scaling down, Greek and American officials approved them. In 1951 construction began, and by 1955 all the major installations had been completed. Italian reparations as well as American aid funds were used to finance the project, which cost altogether $115 million.

The generating stations were established in western Macedonia, in the island of Euboea, in the central Peloponnese and in Epirus. The largest, on Euboea, derived power from local lignite deposits, but the others depended on water power. All but the small plant in Epirus were linked by a power line, which extended from near the Yugoslav border in Macedonia into the Peloponnese. Spur lines were built to reach centers of population that lay along this route. As a result of this construction, Greece had by 1956 more than twice its prewar generating capacity, and since the capacity could now be used far more efficiently than before (when many factories depended on small electric power plants of their own which operated for only eight hours or so of any given day), the actual amount of power generated in 1955 was 5.7 times as great as in 1939. By the end of 1955, 384 communities were connected to the national power grid. All but forty of these had never had electricity before.

Administration of the new power facilities was entrusted to a Public Power Corporation, organized somewhat along the lines of the TVA. Except in Athens-Piraeus, where a British-owned company held a franchise that will not expire for several years to come, the Public Power Corporation bought out local power companies, and instituted a uniform charge for electric power throughout the country. This was a radical departure from former conditions. Electricity in the provinces had previously cost far more than in the capital area, where larger and more efficient installations, together with the fact that the Athens-Piraeus Power Company had the privilege of importing coal duty-free, made cheaper current possible. In many localities, the drop in the price of electricity when the Public Power Corporation came in was extreme, cutting former scales by as much as three quarters or even four fifths.

It was intended, however, that the Public Power Corporation should run its affairs on a profit-making basis, in order to permit accumulation of funds for further construction and extension of the power network. For this reason, power still remained cheaper in the Athens-Piraeus area than elsewhere in Greece, but the differential was nothing like what it had been before. This change certainly reduced one of the obstacles that had previously hindered industrial development outside Athens-Piraeus.

Of all the engineering achievements of the American aid programs in Greece, the construction of a power net was the most dramatic, and promised to be second in importance only to the extension of the road system. Other major undertakings — roads, railroads, and the programs in industry and agriculture — represented either the repair of wartime damages or emergency treatment aimed primarily at short-term results. The electrification program, on the contrary, was something new, and provided the country with one of the basic sinews of industry on a scale never before approached. Much will depend upon the wisdom and technical skill with which the Public Power Corporation conducts its affairs in the future; much will also depend upon the response of businessmen and industrialists to the new opportunities opened by the existence of the power net. So far, their response has been disappointing. Household consumption of electricity has risen markedly, industrial consumption very little. It is, however, still too soon to jump to conclusions as to the long-term results of the electrification program.

Even in 1956, when the national electric transmission line was only a year old, its existence gave Greek economic planners room for maneuver as never before. Civil servants in the economic ministries were eagerly nursing plans to bring a number of hitherto uneconomic natural resources, especially minerals, into production with the help of the new power supply. Capital to finance their plans was still sadly deficient, but the new availability of electric power certainly brought their hopes one step closer to realization. In this sense, the electrification program was an undoubted success.

After 1955, an abundant supply of relatively cheap power removed one of the major handicaps under which Greek industry had long labored. But other difficulties that stood in the way of a smooth and self-sustaining growth of industry were not really overcome, and continued to hamper the national economy. Two difficulties that seemed at least partially remediable through government action were the technical obsolescence of many factories and the failure of private capital to invest significantly in new industry. Up to 1956, official efforts to remedy these shortcomings had not borne much fruit, yet some bold and rather drastic steps were taken after 1952, aimed at improving both conditions; and direct investment by the government in industrial expansion — a program facilitated by the liberalization of American economic aid policy in Greece after 1952 — helped to offset the continued reluctance of private capitalists to build new factories.

To understand how this occurred, it is necessary to know something about the political scene. The unstable coalition governments which emerged from the elections of 1950 pleased nobody, aside from the handful of ministers who held office at any given time. Fresh elections in 1951 did not significantly alter the situation. In 1952, however, after strong pressure from the United States Embassy, and in accordance with a rather widespread sentiment in Greece itself, the electoral system was changed. Instead of proportional representation, designed to give each party a share in the seats of the Chamber of Deputies commensurate with its popular vote, a majority system was instituted, according to which the candidate receiving the largest vote in each constituency was declared elected. The result was to induce most of the party leaders to enter into election coalitions, so that in effect two rival party groupings went to the polls instead of a dozen or more separate parties.

This, by itself, might have made little difference, since party splits and the old style of political intrigue could flourish within a coalition almost as well as between separate parties. But the fact that General Alexander Papagos made himself the leader of one of the coalitions did alter the realities of politics very deeply. Papagos was a man of enormous prestige in Greece. He made his reputation by serving as the commander in chief of the Greek armies both in the Albanian war of 1940–41 and during the victorious phase of the guerrilla war, 1948–49. After retiring from the army in May 1951, [16] he founded a new political

16. The circumstances under which Papagos retired from military life were, to say the least, confused. His somewhat imperious temper had led him into a personal quarrel with King Paul, apparently because some of the King's advisers in the palace were doing things of which Papagos disapproved. Details have never been made public, but enough leaked out at the time to stimulate all sorts of wild rumors.

When the General's resignation was announced, a group of his enthusiastic admirers among the officers of the Athens garrison decided upon a *coup d'état*, but were dissuaded from it by Papagos himself after they had occupied a few government buildings with their troops. The leaders were dismissed from the army, but no other punishment was imposed upon them.

This was the sole occasion after World War II when a military *coup d'état* of a sort that had been endemic in Greece between 1909 and 1936 was attempted. This perhaps mirrors more the privileged position of the Greek armed forces as recipients of American aid than it does any far-reaching change in the psychology of the officer corps. At any rate, rumors of the existence of politically colored secret societies among the officers of the army, navy and air force remained widespread, and may have had some basis in fact.

movement, "The Rally of the Greek People," as a protest against "politics as usual," and made no concessions to the politicians who joined him. As a military man, Papagos was used to giving orders, and he cultivated a manner of cool hauteur that allowed him to overawe the normal quarrelsomeness of politically ambitious Greeks.

The combination of Papagos' personal prestige, his claim to represent a new departure in political life (he had deliberately rejected the soiled name of "party" for his movement), and the operation of the majority electoral system resulted in a resounding victory for his supporters in November 1952. For the first time since the war, Greece acquired a government that had overwhelming support in the Chamber of Deputies, and that, under the stern eye of General Papagos, could and did for a period of more than a year refrain from excessive preoccupation with personal and party intrigue.

This turn of affairs aroused intense satisfaction among American officials in Greece. Here at last, they believed, was a government with which they could do business. Consequently, American purse strings, which had been pulled tight under preceding prime ministers, were unloosed a little. A $10 million loan was arranged to re-endow a reorganized and renamed Central Loan Committee, in order that fresh loans to private businesses might be made. And, as mentioned above, the policy of refusing to consider aid grants for new projects was relaxed, so that the national government began to plan hopefully for the creation of a number of new industrial plants. The first on which work started was an oil refinery situated on the Bay of Salamis near Athens. In addition, road building on a rather large scale was started again, partly to relieve unemployment. It took time to draw up plans such as these in full detail, and it took still more time for all the bureaucratic levels of Greek and American officialdom to act upon them. As a result, it was not until the fiscal year 1954–55 that the relaxation of American official attitudes toward grants for new projects in Greece showed itself in the tangible form of increased aid appropriations. Construction work on most of the projects had just begun in 1956.

Papagos' Rally had come to power on the wings of promises and expectations for prompt and vigorous action. His cabinet was dominated by a ruthless but capable younger man, Spyros Markezinis, Minister of Coordination, who was both a rightist and a radical, ready for drastic action to restore Greece to a stronger position at home and abroad. Such a man found it hard to wait patiently until American officials and the United States Congress had been persuaded to approve and finance his plans. And all of Papagos' ministers, not least Papagos himself, found it galling to be so completely under the thumb of the youthful American economists who staffed the United States mission. An obvious remedy was to find alternative sources of aid.

For their part, the Americans were by no means anxious to maintain a monopoly of the dubious privilege of making loans and grants to Greece, such as they had enjoyed since 1947. When, therefore, Markezinis set out to find other sources of foreign aid, the Americans gave him a cordial blessing. Markezinis met with some success. For example, he was able to arrange a private contract between a Greek firm and Krupp of Germany, whereby the Krupp firm provided credit and access to some of its patents for the erection of a nickel-processing plant near Lamia. Markezinis was also able to arrange for a French government loan to the Public Power Corporation to enable that organization to start building an additional hydroelectric station in central Greece to supplement those already financed through American aid and Italian reparations.

The Krupp contract was the sole example of large-scale private industrial investment in Greece which had passed beyond the stage of preliminary negotiation by 1956. For the rest, the economic policies of the Papagos government amounted to a resumption of the pattern of governmental financing of industrial expansion which had been characteristic of the first postwar period. Moreover, the Papagos government went further than ever before, inasmuch as it did not content itself with making loans to private businessmen but also embarked upon direct governmental construction of a few new industrial plants. This was mildly ironical, since one of the proclaimed principles of the Rally was to encourage private enterprise and to reduce the scope of official regulation of the economy. But when private capital could not be called forth to undertake new investment, Markezinis found no difficulty in putting his principles in his pocket, and went ahead with as much public industrial investment as he could finance.

As far as existing industry was concerned, Markezinis and his collaborators found it possible to act more nearly in accord with their professed convictions. A series of rather radical moves were therefore made to do away with some of the special protection and regulation which had grown up around industry in the preceding decades. The currency was devalued in May 1954, putting internal Greek price levels at or below world prices. The exchange rate for the drachma was again doubled, making it 30,000 to the dollar; but at the same time a new currency was issued, dropping three zeros from the face value of the notes, so that 30 "new" drachmae equaled a dollar. This done, exchange controls were largely dismantled; imports were allowed to come into the country freely except for custom duties, which constituted an important element in the government's revenue, and also, of course, helped to protect home industry from the full rigor of foreign competition. A third step was to remove some of the more galling restrictions which had previously been put upon the operation of foreign corporations.

The theory behind these moves was that Greek industrial firms should be forced to face competition from abroad — forced, that is, to lower prices and modernize machinery, or else go bankrupt. As long as the effect of the currency devaluation remained, this bitter alternative did not actually arise. Freer imports simplified the supply of raw materials to factories, and the low internal price level made it easy at first for domestic firms to meet foreign prices. In a few lines of industry, notably cement, Greece was even able to export. But the Papagos government was not able to halt the steady spiral of inflation. In spite of rather highhanded and sweeping efforts to increase tax yields, directed especially at wealthy persons who had previously escaped their full share of income taxes, revenue still did not match expenditures. Hence by degrees the internal price level crept upward again, until by 1955 Greek factories began to find difficulty in selling their products. This was especially true in textiles, mainly because many of the plants were seriously obsolescent. Statistics compiled by the Greek Federation of Industries showed a decrease of 3.7 per cent in employment in large-scale enterprises, from 82,000 in May 1955 to 79,000 in May 1956. This was almost entirely due to the closing down of a number of textile mills.

This setback interrupted what had been a rather rapid and highly satisfactory rate of industrial and agricultural expansion. Despite the stoppage of the more ambitious investment plans after 1951, indices of production continued to rise until 1955, as the multifarious programs of the first postwar years began to bring tangible returns. The industrial production index of the Greek Federation of Industries, based on 1939 as 100, advanced from 53 in 1946 to 110 in 1950 and 183 in 1955. The Ministry of Agriculture's index of agricultural production was 146 in 1955 as against 100 in 1950, the base year. Figures for 1956 were not yet available when I was in Greece, but the difficulties of the textile industry made it seem improbable that the industrial index would rise much, if at all; and even if the difficulty should prove local and temporary, the general deceleration of investment since 1951 will almost certainly mean a slower rate of growth in the immediate future.

Just as the economic situation was thus becoming troublesome once more, Papagos died, in October 1955, after an illness of several months. Even before his death, the Rally he had created showed signs of disintegration, as quarrels broke out among Papagos' would-be political heirs. In the event, the King chose a comparatively young and previously inconspicuous politician, Constantine Karamanlis, to become prime minister upon Papagos' death. Karamanlis then proceeded to organize a new party of his own, and called for elections in February 1956. Although his supporters polled a minority of the total vote, they won a small majority in the Chamber of Deputies, thanks to some unscrupulous but very skillful gerrymandering of electoral districts on the eve of the election.

In spite of Karamanlis' victory, therefore, Greece no longer enjoyed the advantage of a solidly based government that could afford to risk unpopular measures. The genuinely radical tinge which had colored Papagos' movement in its first days was gone, and "politics as usual" began once more to prevail. One sign of the changed spirit (which emerged some months before Papagos' death) was that the government decided to raise a number of tariffs in order to protect hard-pressed home industries. The radical cure of Papagos' first days had to be abandoned or at least modified since home industry, instead of becoming more efficient under the pressure of foreign competition, showed signs of folding up.

One reason the retreat seemed necessary was that little or no progress had been made in meeting another great and persistent

obstacle to industrial development. Private capital remained as
shy as ever of investment in industry. Many reasons were here
at work, but one of the major factors inhibiting private industrial investment was the deep-seated unwillingness of the small
man to entrust his hard-won savings to the hands of industrial
managers whom he could not personally control. He much preferred to do something with his money himself.

This might not have been so bad if private savings had taken
the form of bank deposits, for then bank loans might have been
made to industry on the strength of such deposits. But this was
not the case. After having lived through two sky-high inflations
within twenty years, no Greek was willing to keep his money in
a bank. Instead, he put any surplus he acquired into gold coins
— normally British sovereigns or French Napoleons, of which
something like twenty million were estimated to exist in the
country. The gold was then simply hoarded until such time as
enough had accumulated to dower a daughter or build a house
or undertake some similar enterprise of family moment. The
effect, therefore, was to rule out investment in modern factories for all but the handful of very rich persons who might
have enough money to own the new enterprise outright, or at
least be sure of an effective controlling voice in its management.
But such persons were rare, and most of them found shipown-
ing or some other form of investment more attractive. As a result, the real if slender private capital of Greece remained industrially sterile.

The one economic use which the ordinary citizen was prepared to make of his gold was to build himself a house. As a
result, after 1950 and especially after 1952, a great building
boom developed in Athens and in some of the other large
towns. Investment in industry actually declined during the
same period. Housing was undoubtedly needed, but it was

more than doubtful whether the economy could really afford to divert so large a proportion of its capital resources into brick and mortar.

In May 1956, the government introduced a new device to try to lure private capital into the industrial market. The rate of interest on ordinary bank deposits was set at 10 per cent per annum, a figure which, it was hoped, would more than counterbalance inflation, and lure small savings into the banks, where they could be used for industrial and other economically productive loans. Whether this policy will be successful remains to be seen. During the first six months, results were not spectacular, although private bank accounts did increase from almost nothing to the equivalent of $62 million.

By comparison with the somewhat precarious condition of industry, agriculture went ahead relatively smoothly and steadily, without requiring much special attention from the government. Slow but uninterrupted progress in increasing the area under irrigation was made, partly through bank loans extended to individual farmers or to village cooperatives, and partly by direct government construction. Between 1950 and 1955, a total of 120,000 acres were newly irrigated. This amounted to almost 1.3 per cent of all the cultivated area of the country, and was therefore far from insignificant. The rise of fertilizer consumption continued, and new crops and methods introduced to the farmers by the agricultural extension agents did their bit to increase yields.

With these programs proceeding satisfactorily on the whole, the government turned attention to an old problem: land reform. In 1952 a law was passed making it illegal for any one person to own more than 400 stremmata (100 acres) of crop land. Land in excess of this maximum was to be sold, and state officials were to superintend the transactions. According to the official estimate of the Ministry of Agriculture, about half a million acres changed ownership as a result of this law; but in many cases it appears that landowners succeeded in retaining effective control of their estates by lodging title to their excess properties in the hands of some friend or relative who could be counted upon not to assert the normal rights of ownership. The law, therefore, does not seem to have been of much consequence. In general, the countryside still remains, as it has been for a generation, a land of small peasant holdings. Larger farms conducted on a commercial basis with hired labor are few and isolated.

The American aid programs and the efforts the people of Greece made to help themselves, while they fell far short of the rosier hopes and more ambitious goals which had been set at the beginning, nevertheless sufficed to keep Greek society and government from the collapse into revolution which so clearly threatened in 1947, and brought about a prompt and substantial increase in almost every type of economic activity. Statistically it can be shown that between 1949 and 1956 Greece successfully began to readjust the disbalance between population and developed resources which for the preceding fifty years or more had constituted the basic source of social and political instability within the nation. During these years, the development of the economy, instead of lagging behind population growth as it did in the first part of this century, definitely took the lead. This meant that the average Greek had a chance to live at least as well as his father and perhaps a bit better. But in practice, of course, the incidence of such statistical averages was uneven. Some individuals and some regions forged far ahead, while others remained caught in the old vicious circle of more and more mouths and less and less food for any one of them.

To appreciate this side of recent Greek development, we must look at a few more or less representative villages, and at the experiences of varying sorts of people in the towns. For no matter how successful American aid and Greek effort have been in raising total production and in improving statistical averages, it is obvious that the fundamental aim — to create a stable and self-sustaining society and economy — will not have been achieved if the growing prosperity of some segments of the population simply sets off more sharply the progressive impoverishment of other groups. Shared suffering, like shared prosperity, may consolidate social feelings; it is when some prosper while others do not that the strains upon social cohesion are greatest. For this reason we shall turn to specific cases, to illustrate the discrepancies of economic growth that have appeared in the last few years.

WARTIME REFUGEES

Supported by government rations and relief payments, these women and their children had been living in this large tent for two years when this picture was taken in 1949. At the height of the guerrilla war almost one tenth of the people of Greece were living in conditions like these. Resettlement and rehabilitation of refugees was the most urgent problem facing Greek officials and the American aid mission when hostilities ended late in 1949.

ROAD BUILDING

Villagers in the Grammos Mountains of western Macedonia buildin a new spur road to connect their village with the main road system The new soft dirt road will enable the village to exploit its fore resources, and these in turn will provide increased tax revenue to pc for the road. Since 1949, approximately 1,500 miles of simple di roads have been constructed, opening almost all the villages of Greec to wheeled traffic. Possibly the most fundamental of the great change wrought by the American aid program was the construction of second and third-class roads and the improvement of the trunk highway system By 1951 the basic transport system of Greece was not only restored its prewar level but was in much better shape than ever before.

Men and children turn out to celebrate the event as the final connection is made which will bring electricity to the village. The village priest, in ceremonial robes (right foreground), gives his blessing to the occasion. The villagers' clothing compares favorably with that of the power company men in the foreground, but their tile-roofed houses are in poor condition.

LARGE-SCALE INDUSTRY

A view (upper left) of the largest of four electric power stations built by an American engineering firm to provide current for the new national grid. This plant, serving the Athens area and other communities, is operated with lignite obtained from nearby deposits.

The cement industry, one of the most efficient prewar industries of Greece, has provided some exports in recent years, chiefly to countries in the Middle East. The plant of the Titan Cement Company pictured at lower left is at Eleusis, near Athens. Men and women are seen loading cement into a barge, emptying the bags for future use.

The nickel-processing plant pictured below was constructed recently near the city of Lamia in central Greece, by a Greek firm to German specifications and with German capital. Export of partly refined metal was getting under way in the summer of 1956. This plant, completely modern and technically efficient, is the only large enterprise that has been financed by private capital since the end of the war.

A VILLAGE CAFENEION
IN CRETE

A group of mountaineers enjoy their leisure at the *cafeneion*.
One of them (center) plays a three-stringed instrument resembling a violin. Their attire, a free mixture of the traditional
Cretan mountain costume with European clothing, contrasts with
the conservatism of the woman's apparel. During the slack seasons on the farms, Greek villagers spend many hours in village
coffee houses or taverns, discussing politics or exchanging gossip.

Farmers plowing wheat fields in the plain of Thessaly. Mule teams and steel plows have now replaced oxen and wooden plows nearly everywhere in Greece.

AGRICULTURE

Wheat is harvested by an age-old method in the picture at left below. The scene is highly characteristic of the Mediterranean climate zone. A sharp line separates barren hillside and fertile bottom land, and the village, seen in the distance (circled), perches on the fringe of the plain.

At the right below, women weed rice fields in reclaimed salt swamp land. One of the most dramatically successful innovations of agricultural technicians attached to the United States aid mission, paddy rice cultivation has provided work and a new crop for export.

SALONIKA
WATERFRONT

The modern face of Greece's second city is seen in this view of the Salonika waterfront. The high-masted vessels attest to the continued importance of small coastal
shipping. In the far background is the main harbor for oceangoing ships.

CHAPTER 3

THE VILLAGES

Since most of the people of Greece still live in villages, peasant life constitutes something of a base level for Greek society. Pressure of population is felt first and most acutely in the villages. Peasant boys from land-hungry villages are driven to seek a livelihood in the towns, thus creating a pool of unskilled but eager labor which deeply affects the conditions of life among the urban working classes. Moreover, agricultural products are the country's major items of export. What happens in the villages therefore fixes limits upon the general prosperity and social stability of the entire national community. It follows that the best criterion by which to measure the impact of American aid programs on Greek society is to examine what has been accomplished in a few typical villages, for only after the agrarian problems of the nation have been somewhat relieved can there be much expectation of enriching or improving urban conditions.

Two general dividing lines separate the villages of Greece. By far the most important is the contrast, explained in Chapter 1, between hill and plain, that is, between food-deficit and food-surplus rural communities. A second general distinction is between those villages that underwent radical redistribution of land after World War I, and those where patterns of landownership have evolved piecemeal and privately without any massive governmental intervention. Generally, villages of the first type lie in the plains of the north, while all hill villages, and plains villages south of Thessaly, fall into the second category. In view of these important differences, it is necessary to study at least one village from each of these groupings.

Another point of distinction is the degree to which traditional patterns of village life underwent change during the past ten years. Some villages, whether by accident or thanks to intelligent and energetic leadership within the village, were able to undertake quite radical changes and profited very greatly from new techniques of agriculture. Others stayed generally within traditional frames. Still others were able to make only halfway satisfactory changes in old customs and techniques. It seems wise to try to illustrate different degrees of adjustment and improvement, first among plains villages, then among hill villages; and in each case to begin with an example of slight change and conclude with an example of maximally successful adjustment.

Before turning to an account of what particular villages have done, however, it might be well to say something about village leadership, and the relations between villagers and officials of the national government. Until 1951, the villages (and larger communities) were governed by appointees of the Ministry of Interior. This sometimes led to disharmony and distrust between the inhabitants and their legal representatives. In 1951, however, elections were organized in villages (and larger communities), so that for the first time since the war the people had a chance to choose their own local officials. Villagers elect members of the village council, which varies in size with the size of the community. The council members then choose one of their number as president and another as secretary.

The secretary's duty is to keep village records; but the main responsibilities rest upon the president. He represents the village in all dealings with the outer world, and has an informal authority to hear complaints and settle quarrels within the village. Legal cases, however, lie beyond his competence; they are dealt with by regular judges, appointed by the Ministry of Justice.

A second center of village leadership is the church. Every village has a church, and the priest is often a native of the village, distinguished from his fellows by a special garb and the fact that he has attended a seminary for a year or longer. Priests are appointed by bishops, but a congregation has the right to refuse a nomination, or to object to a priest it dislikes. In such cases the bishop normally attempts to find someone else to suit the wishes of the community.

A third focus of leadership is the school system. Nearly every village has a primary school, staffed by a teacher who has had at least a secondary school education. Unlike the priest or the president, he is most often a stranger to the community, appointed to his post by the Ministry of Education. Here, in many villages, lies an important point of contact with the outside world; but just because the schoolmaster is usually an outsider and often a city man, he fails to command in most villages quite the same trust and authority that the priest and president enjoy.

As one would expect in any small community whose members are acquainted from childhood, the effectiveness of formal leadership depends very much upon the personalities of the office holders. In some villages, the president and secretary have little real importance. As a minimum, they must keep records to allow the army to draft the young men when their age group is called up, and it is their duty to muster the able-bodied villagers for a fixed number of days' labor on roads or other public works when ordered to do so by officials of the central government. This labor service is the only form of direct taxation now enforced upon peasants, and money payment may be substituted for personal service if anyone cares to do so.

Only when a village chooses to undertake local improvements requiring money or supplies from outside sources does the sphere of local government expand from this legal minimum. In such cases, the village president, perhaps assisted by some other members of the council, is expected to represent the village in all dealings with the agents of the central government from whom help is sought; and if the village contracts a corporate loan for some project, then the president becomes responsible for collecting the sums needed to repay the loan.

Generally, the villagers of Greece have a deep-seated and not altogether groundless distrust of outsiders, particularly of government representatives, whom they suspect of being more often out to fleece than to help them. Long and persistent persuasion is therefore usually required on the part of government officials to overcome this suspicion, and open the way for technical or other improvements in village life. More often than not, the initiative in bringing about the changes which have come to many villages in the past ten years came from outside the village, from the central government. Only after a start had been made, and the practical advantage of some new crop or technique had been demonstrated on a small scale, did the farmers

crowd around for advice, loans, seed and the like, and begin
to turn to their local village government for assistance in bringing further improvements to the community.

Let us now turn to specific cases, and see what has happened
in six representative villages during the past ten years.

Villages of the Plains

LOFISCOS

Lofiscos is situated in the plain of Thessaly, about half a mile
off the main trunk road between Larissa and Volos. This is a
region of hot summers and cold winters, for Thessaly is land-
locked, surrounded west, east and south by precipitous mountains, and exposed to cold northern winds coming down from
the plateau of western Macedonia in winter. It is the best wheat
land of Greece, and wheat is the major — indeed almost the
sole — crop raised by the villagers of Lofiscos today.

As the visitor approaches the village over a wandering track,
deeply rutted by trucks that traverse the soft earth during the
muddy months of winter and spring, Lofiscos looks shabby and
ill-kempt. Houses are scattered irregularly; little fresh paint is
in evidence. The dominant structure near the center of the village is a half-ruined rectangular stone tower that looks like and
in fact once was a small fortress.

Before 1881, the year in which Thessaly was annexed to
Greece, this building was inhabited by a Turkish pasha, who
owned the entire area which now belongs to the villagers of
Lofiscos. The ground floor was his granary and stable; in the
upper story the great man lived with his harem. Since 1881 the
building has been abandoned and allowed to decay slowly. The
scattered huts in which the villagers live also survive from
Turkish times in almost every case. The inhabitants are the

sons or grandsons of men who once tilled the Turk's lands for him on a sharecropping basis. They stayed behind when the Turk departed, and in due course fell heir to his land.

These changes did not happen all at once. When the Turkish landowner left he sold his rights to a wealthy Greek who lived in Larissa. The new landlord continued the old arrangements, with the difference that he was an absentee. Early in the twentieth century, however, widespread peasant unrest manifested itself in Thessaly, and in 1912 a law of expropriation was passed against the large landowners. But it was not until 1920 that the effect of this law was felt in Lofiscos. In that year government surveyors and officials carried out a general distribution of the estate. Every male resident of the village nineteen years old or over was given possession of 137 stremmata of land (34¼ acres). In addition, 15 stremmata (3¾ acres) were assigned to each male member of a community of semi-migratory shepherds who had immemorially used these lands for winter pasture, paying a fee to the owner for the privilege of grazing their sheep on the stubble left after the grain harvest. A thousand stremmata (250 acres) remained in the possession of the absentee landowner. The rest of the land was left as common pasture. Much of it was unsuited to cultivation because of flooding in the spring; and in any case 137 stremmata was about all the land a single family could easily cultivate with the tools then available to them.

The land settlement of 1920 remained essentially unchanged thereafter. Many of the men who received their farms at that time are still alive; five families had moved into the village by 1956, but no one had moved away. The five newcomers owned no land at all, but worked for the established farmers of the village or, more often, on the big estate of the absentee owner. (Incidentally, this estate survived in 1956 as a working unit in spite of the land law of 1952 which forbade ownership of more than 400 stremmata of cultivated land. Presumably the owner had divided legal title among relatives or friends without surrendering real control of his land.)

The village is very small. In 1956 its population was only 130,[1] yet it occupies no less than 6,000 acres, excluding the absentee landowner's estate, which is counted as part of the lands of Lofiscos by official government reckoning. This amounts to more than 46 acres per capita; and even though more than half of the land remains rough pasture, subject to flooding for part of every year, such an abundance of land represents solid wealth by Greek peasant standards. And indeed, the village is wealthy. Farmers find little difficulty in accumulating gold sovereigns with which to dower their daughters, for wheat is always in demand and a government purchase scheme keeps the price stable and well above world market levels. In spite of the shabby appearance of their houses and the untidy appearance of their clothes, the families of Lofiscos are, by their own standards, very well off. Almost all of them probably have several hundred gold sovereigns hidden away, but this no stranger could ever expect to know.

The tribulations of the second world war, of the occupation and of the guerrilla war made almost no impression on Lofiscos. The young men served in the army, of course, and saw something of the outer world. But on their return they seemed to fit back smoothly into the familiar routine. As the guerrillas never

1. This and all subsequent figures for village populations are rough approximations. Village records do not include any sort of census figure. They are confined to registration of births, marriages and deaths, and the most important function they serve is to provide the basis for the annual call-up of military recruits. Moreover, a family often remains registered in a village long after it has moved away; in such instances births and deaths are likely to be omitted from the village books, and may or may not be recorded elsewhere. One must therefore depend upon informal estimates of village officials. This leaves a considerable margin for error, unless the officials consulted are unusually careful.

penetrated so far into the heart of the Thessalian plain, the villagers saw nothing of them at first hand. Life went on smoothly, and the market for wheat was good. In general, then, the tenor of life in Lofiscos is a thoroughly conservative one. In 1920 the villagers attained their hearts' desire — possession of the land; and since then nothing has happened to make them wish to change the way they live.

The general conservatism of the village is reflected in the caution with which the farmers have taken up new techniques and ideas. There was no pressing economic necessity to impel them to experiment. Familiar methods and crops did well enough. Yet there are at present real signs of technical change. In 1952 fertilizer came in for the first time. Up till then no one in the village had used it. In that year, a representative of the Agricultural Bank visited the village, and urged the farmers to buy fertilizer on credit. A few of them made the experiment; the results they achieved convinced all the rest, for with fertilizer the wheat crop was nearly twice what had been usual before. Every farmer is now using fertilizer, and the net production of the fields is rising accordingly.

Then in 1956 a single farmer, more venturesome than his fellows, contracted a five-year loan with the Agricultural Bank in order to install a well and pump with which to irrigate four acres. This represented a far greater departure from custom than the use of fertilizer. Wheat does not need irrigation in Thessaly, and to repay the cost of the well and pump new crops had to be introduced. Cotton was the answer, and the results in 1956, when I visited the village, were already so promising that several other farmers were planning to install a well-pump irrigation system in their fields, and grow cotton the next year. By doing so they can multiply their cash yield per acre several times as compared to the traditional income from wheat farming. This prospect is all the farmers need to persuade them to go ahead.

While I did not come to know the village well enough to be sure, my impression was that the decisive break-through in 1952 was not a matter of new knowledge or information so much as a change in financial attitudes. That is to say, before 1952 the peasants of Lofiscos looked upon indebtedness with horror. Anyone who went to a bank and of his own free will incurred a debt was, they felt, courting disaster. This was not far from the case in the 1920's and early 1930's when agricultural prices were uncertain, bank interest high, and foreclosure a possibility. In 1956 bank interest was still high — between 7 and 8 per cent for loans to individual farmers — but the price of wheat was fixed ahead of time by the government, and the price of fertilizer had been lowered by government subsidy. As a result, a simple computation could assure the borrower of what he stood to gain. This was what the farmers of Lofiscos learned in 1952. They allowed the Bank's representative to convince them that there were times and circumstances when borrowing was not the first step to perdition, but a sure (or nearly sure) way to greater income.

Farming in Lofiscos has always, for as long as men can recall, been mainly directed at market sale. Wheat from the village has gone to Volos or Larissa year after year, and, since 1920 at least, the peasants have been able to buy town products as they wanted them. But in general they have preferred hoarding to spending. In Turkish times, to build a comfortable new house or to dress elaborately would simply have attracted the attention of some hungry tax or rent collector; hence there was a strong motive for concealing behind an unpretentious, indeed poor-seeming, exterior any wealth that might accumulate. This attitude apparently survived under Greek administration, even after the peasants of the village ceased to owe rents to a landlord and secured the whole harvest as their own. It still lingers: hence the shabby appearance of the village and its inhabitants.

If the first important break with old traditional patterns of life in Lofiscos dates only from 1952, it cannot be surprising to find that as yet little has altered outwardly. But since the village has been attuned to a market economy for generations, and since changes that increase income without involving more than the normal risks of farming meet with little resistance in the village, it seems entirely probable that in the future more and more substantial changes will come to Lofiscos. In 1956 there was still much that could be done to increase the intensity of farming and to enlarge the cash income of the farmers. Well irrigation is easy, because the water table lies close to the surface; and with such irrigation, a wide variety of hitherto untried crops will become possible: vegetables, fruit, fodder, in addition to cotton. The basis for a highly productive and diversified farming may thus appear in a relatively short period of time. Moreover, it would not be difficult or very expensive to build drainage works in the portion of the village lands that flood each spring, thus bringing some or all of that land into cultivation.

Two obstacles stand in the path of any such program of development in Lofiscos. One is the general inertia and conservatism of the farmers, who will have to learn a good deal about new crops and farming methods, and may also find themselves working a good deal more steadily through the year than was necessary when nearly all their land was still in wheat. Yet the means and incentive to overcome this difficulty both seemed to be present in 1956. Agricultural extension agents and the Agricultural Bank stand ready to give expert advice and instruction; and some of the farmers of Losfiscos have shown an eagerness to enrich themselves thereby.

The second problem is more complicated. If the farmers begin to exploit the possibilities of their land more fully, the village will very soon find itself short of labor, for the existing inhabitants are too few to attend to all the chores of high farming on so much land. Purchase of machinery, like that used on American farms, would be one way to solve this difficulty; hiring labor from outside the village would be another, and more probable, course. It is conceivable, however, that the villagers of Lofiscos may hesitate about bringing in strangers to work for them. There is a considerable feeling of clannishness among the villagers, a clannishness perhaps reflecting their knowledge that they are far, far better off than the great majority of their fellows, and a desire to keep what they know to be a good thing strictly to themselves. It will not be surprising if, a few years from now, reluctance to hire outside labor begins to hold back the development of more intensive farming in Lofiscos. But if and when the farmers do begin to offer jobs to poor men from the hills, some of the communities that have hitherto seen little benefit from the rising prosperity of villages like Lofiscos will begin to share at least a little in the economic advance of the plains.

All these possibilities lie in the future. In 1956 the village was supplying all its own labor and was just beginning to alter traditional ways. Few villages in Greece are so comfortably situated, and fewer still have such possibilities for further enrichment.

NEA ELEFTHEROHORI

Nea Eleftherohori lies at the foot of Mount Olympus, facing the Thermaic Gulf, about twenty miles north of Katerini, the local market center and regional metropolis. The name means New Free Village, and is a reminder of the fact that there is an older "Free Village" perched high on the slopes of Olympus. In Turkish times, which lasted in this region until 1912, the men of the older Eleftherohori engaged in a little farming but for the most part depended for their living on the sale of firewood and on summer work as carpenters.

The land now occupied by the villagers of Nea Eleftherohori was owned by a Turkish landlord until 1912, and worked by a group of Turkish peasants. These were harried from the land when the Greek army came north in the first Balkan war of 1912. Thereupon, some of the inhabitants of Eleftherohori, together with a large group from another similar hill village, called Katophigi, simply squatted on the vacant land. They apportioned the booty on a first-come, first-served basis, effective title depending on tillage of particular fields. Since there was plenty of land for everyone, this provoked no difficulty.

The situation was radically changed and legally stabilized in 1927 when government authorities surveyed and redistributed village property. The Greek government was then engaged in settling as many as possible of the refugees who had come from Asia Minor in 1922 and 1923 on land vacated by Turks; but it was not deemed politic to drive the squatters entirely away from what they had seized. Consequently, an estimate of the fertility of the soil was made in order to determine the smallest allotment on which a single family could subsist. In Nea Eleftherohori, the allotment was fixed at 27 stremmata, i.e., 6¾ acres. To permit as many refugees as possible to find land, it was further decided that lots would be assigned only to heads of families, not, as had been done earlier in Lofiscos, to every man, married or single.

As far as the squatters, or "old settlers," were concerned, these policies did not usually involve much loss. To be sure, their holdings were reassigned and particular pieces of land changed hands, but possession was so recent that this in itself did not rouse serious resentment. Moreover, few families failed to get as much land as they had previously occupied. When it became known that only heads of families could qualify for an allotment, all the boys of marriageable age, even if only seventeen or eighteen years old, hastened to find themselves wives, and thus made good a claim for 27 stremmata. The original squatters' rights had been apportioned on the basis of the amount of land actually tilled by a given family, and as a man or a boy could scarcely cultivate more than about 27 stremmata single-handed with the sort of equipment they had, the old families received about as much land as they had had before. The difference was that the sons escaped from parental control earlier than they would otherwise have done, since title to their share of the land was now vested individually, not, as traditionally, in the parental family as a whole.

The squatters of 1912 had not occupied all the cultivable land. When they had all received their lots, therefore, almost an equal number of refugees, mostly from the Caucasus area, were settled on the remainder. The two groups stood more or less apart, especially at the beginning. Many of the customs of the Caucasus people seemed wild and barbarous to the old settlers. But because the old settlers felt little or no sense of grievance, and because each family was very nearly on a level of economic equality, with 27 stremmata apiece, the fissure between the two groups was not great. Nevertheless, the houses of the old settlers are still separated by about one hundred yards from those occupied by the refugees, so that the village is physically divided into two quite distinct parts.

In 1932 a supplementary land distribution took place, giving families with more than four members an additional 5 stremmata; in 1937 a further adjustment was made when forty-three families removed to a newly drained area in the valley of the Aliakmon River, and left their allotments behind, to be reassigned in chunks of 5 stremmata to the larger families of Nea Eleftherohori. No further official changes have since been made, but the natural processes of death and inheritance have resulted in the splitting up of a few of the allotments into smaller farms, while in some cases formerly separate allotments have been combined into one holding. The great majority of the families of the village, however, still occupied 27 or 32 stremmata in 1956, and most of the original holders of the allotments were still alive.

The land settlement in Nea Eleftherohori differed from that in Lofiscos in two respects. First, the farms in Nea Eleftherohori were less than one fifth as large as in Lofiscos. Second, the new settlers, uprooted from their former homes, whether up the mountain or in distant Asia Minor, left binding customary ways of life behind them, and started off in Nea Eleftherohori without the automatic conservatism and suspicion of innovation typical until very recently of the families of Lofiscos. These differences acted together to make the farmers of Nea Eleftherohori a good deal more willing to try new crops and methods, even before the war, than those in the older Thessalian community. Life on so little land was difficult at best, and anything that promised to bring in a little more seemed worth trying; and when the problems of farming the land were new in any event, there was far less psychological resistance against trying some further innovation.

Another contrast with Lofiscos, a contrast perhaps related to the general shake-up of old customary routines which came to the inhabitants of Nea Eleftherohori between 1912 and 1923, is that the new settlers proceeded to procreate children at a far greater rate than occurs in Lofiscos, where families are mostly quite small. [2]

2. It would be very interesting to know why the prosperous peasants of Lofiscos have fewer children than their much poorer fellows in Nea Eleftherohori, but I do not know Lofiscos well enough to hazard an opinion. Can it be that the general market orientation of their agriculture and the habit of calculating in monetary terms leads them to restrict the number of their children deliberately, in some fashion or other, realizing that to divide the family farm among many children spells impoverishment for

The smallness of the original farms and the large size of most families in Nea Eleftherohori began, even in the late 1930's, to present the villagers with a very serious problem. What were their children going to do? To divide the land was a desperate solution, inasmuch as the farms were already near the minimum that a single family could subsist upon. Somehow or other, all but one son had to be freed from the land, find some other form of livelihood, and leave the entire farm to be inherited by one brother. Hopeless poverty if not outright hunger was the certain lot of everyone who stayed on a divided inheritance. [3]

Nea Eleftherohori has been less fortunate than Lofiscos in still another respect. Situated at the foot of Mount Olympus, it lay just on the edge of the territory that guerrilla bands controlled in 1943–45 and again in 1947–49. These were, therefore, years of intense political insecurity in the village, and some loss of life. In 1947 the guerrillas organized a raid upon Nea Elef-

the new generation? If so, why not in Nea Eleftherohori? To be sure, that village pursued a more nearly subsistence style of agriculture between the wars; but this fact by itself does not seem enough to explain the contrast. Perhaps the prevalence of early marriages in Nea Eleftherohori, consequent upon the mode of land distribution in 1927, accounts for the difference, early marriages naturally bringing larger families; or perhaps some recklessness engendered by the catastrophic upheaval which the Asia Minor refugee population underwent encouraged large families, for there is in Nea Eleftherohori, as in all of Greece, a noticeable differential in birth rate between refugee and "old settler" groups, with the refugees standing higher.

3. In legal form, the Greek government retained title to all the land distributed to refugees and squatters after World War I. Part of the original justification for this policy was that it would permit the government to prevent excessive subdivision of peasant farms; and it was still the case in 1956 that legal tenure of each allotment was lodged in a single family head. This, however, did not prevent some families from dividing the allotments in practice among the heirs. Yet the fact that such divisions could not be legalized may perhaps have reinforced the reluctance of the families of Nea Eleftherohori to make them.

therohori and plundered an UNRRA storehouse which had been set up there. This was bad enough from the point of view of the villagers; but what was far more awkward was the fact that sentiment was seriously divided within the village itself. Approximately half the population sympathized more or less completely with the guerrillas, and in 1947–48 about twenty young men and women from the village fought in their ranks. Only three of them returned. In 1947, when I first visited Nea Eleftherohori, the atmosphere was exceedingly tense. No one was quite sure of his neighbor, and no one was sure whether the government or the guerrillas would win in the end. Armed men patrolled the village at night on behalf of the government, and felt free to pay disconcerting calls upon families known or believed to be sympathetic with the guerrillas. Fifteen persons were arrested by the nearby gendarmes after the raid of 1947, and one of them was executed; the rest returned only after two and a half years of detention. The general mood of the village at that time was one of fear and frustration. No one could see any solution to the difficulties of the present, still less those of the future. What could the young boys do who were not needed at home? With no land available in the village, and no jobs obtainable in town, the situation seemed nearly hopeless.

By 1956 the outlook had changed. First of all, the political division within the village had healed over, leaving almost no trace. The renewed solidarity of village feeling dated from 1950, when the president and council of the community — who, as appointees of the Ministry of Interior, were of course leading anti-Communists — asked the local police to release two of the village boys who had returned from serving with the guerrillas and had been arrested on general suspicion. The police acted favorably upon this request, and allowed their prisoners to go free without further punishment. This affair, which showed a degree of magnanimity on the part of the anti-Communist leaders of the village since a son of one of them had been caught and killed in a guerrilla ambush near the village during the war, inaugurated a new era in Nea Eleftherohori. Everyone felt relieved that old feuds were not to be pursued, and made haste to forget the quarrels that had so long divided the village.

More important, or at least more promising for the long run, was that after 1950 the villagers began to see some hope of a solution to their long-range difficulties. This hope was based on two innovations. They began to send nearly all their younger sons to secondary school, hoping thereby to qualify them for jobs in town, away from the land. And they began to intensify their farming and to increase their cash income by raising market crops on a far greater scale than before.

The path to higher education was greatly facilitated by the proximity of a gymnasium (i.e., a "classical" high school), located in a large village about ten miles away. A bus service was instituted between Nea Eleftherohori and the school, enabling boys from the village to attend classes and still live at home. Since there were no tuition fees, secondary school education became comparatively cheap; though even so, the cost of books and other supplies was, for many families, a serious matter. By 1956 no fewer than thirty-six boys from Nea Eleftherohori were attending the gymnasium. This number included almost every boy of appropriate age who had an elder brother, that is, almost every boy who would not inherit a farm. Roughly one third of all the families of the village had a boy in the gymnasium.

Since 1950, a number of changes in farming methods have also occurred. The first was the use of fertilizer. A few farmers had experimented with it before the war, but it cost so much that they found that in a year of bad or only middling weather they could not make enough on the extra yield of their fields to pay off the debt incurred to buy it. Hence use of fertilizer was abandoned, to be resumed only in 1950. By 1956 "everybody" was using fertilizer, and yields of wheat (the principal crop for which fertilizer was needed) had increased to between 125 and 180 okes per stremma, as against the former range of 60 to 80, depending of course on weather and variations in the quality of the land.

Even before the war, the farmers of Nea Eleftherohori had shown themselves willing to try new crops. Thus in 1947 there were modest acreages in legumes, cotton and tobacco as well as some vegetables. Only tobacco did well, since there was no irrigation; but government regulations forbade extension of tobacco acreage, in order to maintain prices. By 1956 this restriction had been removed for the district in which Nea Eleftherohori is situated, and the farmers promptly began to increase their tobacco planting. In 1947 there had been a total of 52 stremmata in tobacco; in 1955 there were 480, and in 1956 no less than 898. Tobacco has in fact become the main labor-consuming crop, and it has also become the all-important cash crop for the village. Money income has multiplied several times over with the spread of tobacco cultivation, for earlier, when wheat, raised without benefit of fertilizer, was the main crop, there was often very little left to sell after the families had supplied their own food needs.

A second major departure occurred in 1956. With the help of a bank loan, the village planted an olive grove on 900 stremmata of rough pasture. It will take ten years for the new trees to come into full production; but when they do, Nea Eleftherohori will have a new and valuable crop, with the special virtue of requiring labor at a season of the year when other agricultural operations are more or less at a standstill. By combining grain farming (requiring labor in the early fall for planting and in the late spring for the harvest) with tobacco raising (requiring intensive labor in the early spring and for about two months in the late summer when the leaves must be picked daily and strung up to dry) and olives (harvested in the late fall and the early winter), the village will be able to distribute its labor over nearly the entire round of the year, and minimize the long seasonal idleness which was characteristic of its older grain-centered type of agriculture.

Another way of describing what has happened in Nea Eleftherohori is to say that during the past five or six years commercial agriculture has largely supplanted a primarily subsistence type of agriculture. Related to this development is a very great change in the appearance of the village and of its inhabitants. Increased money income, deriving from tobacco, has been spent, in part, for city-type clothes, which every self-respecting villager has by now acquired. In part, too, money has been used to fix up the houses, which now appear very clean and tidy. Almost all have been freshly painted or whitewashed, and several families have fenced in tidy yards where a vine trellis gives shade from the sun. On the surface, Nea Eleftherohori appears far more prosperous than Lofiscos. Apparently, a fairly high level of housekeeping has become standard in Nea Eleftherohori, and a great effort is made by almost everyone to present a good front to the neighbors.

The refugees from Asia Minor constitute a partial exception to this rule. Their houses are somewhat shabbier, their dress perceptibly poorer. The old settlers look down upon them as careless farmers and poor housekeepers. The differences are not really great, but the desire to keep ahead of the refugees has probably acted as an important spur to laggard or lazy members of the old settler group, forcing them to improve their homes and to dress better than they might otherwise have done.

Indeed, if I understood the spirit of the village correctly, the desire to maintain a status and keep a respectable front to the world has become the overriding aim of the whole community. One very important consequence is the postponement of marriages. Until the means for living respectably can be assured, the families of Nea Eleftherohori are no longer willing to allow their children to marry, nor do the children themselves wish it. In 1956, a young man who would inherit a farm of 27 stremmata expected his bride to bring with her a dowry of about 300 gold pounds. This is a truly extraordinary figure for any family in the village to raise, equal to $3,000 in American currency and considerably more in local purchasing power. Ten or fifteen years of strenuous saving are required to accumulate so much, all the more since appearances have to be maintained in the meantime, and this takes money too. Consequently, a good many men and women in their thirties and some in their early forties remain unmarried.

Once again, a partial exception must be made for the refugees, among whom the dowry system is not so universal and binding as among the old settlers, and who still sometimes marry young and before the new family has any assured means of support. But the dowry system is said to be spreading among them too; and the disdain (mingled perhaps with a certain envy) with which the old settlers speak of the refugees' irresponsible marriages makes it clear that the strongest sort of social pressure is at work to prevent such occurrences.

Apparently the people of Nea Eleftherohori are making use of an old custom, the dowry, to regulate population growth. Quite consciously and deliberately, they seek to keep their numbers within the limits imposed by their economic position; or, to put it the other way around, the villagers are determined not to sink into poverty, or to allow their children to do so; and by postponing marriages they know they can avoid the disaster of having too many mouths to feed.

The birth records of the village show what has been accomplished in this direction. Before 1939 the number of births annually recorded never sank below 42, and went as high as 77 in 1933. Since the war the number of recorded births has never exceeded 19, and sank as low as 11 in 1953. Deaths have declined also, but not as sharply, so that the natural increase of the village population in the early 1950's ranged from 6 to 12 persons a year instead of the 30 to 40 a year of the early 1930's. This decrease is the more striking since the total population of the village grew from something like 450 at the time the basic distribution of land was made in 1927 to 875 in 1956.

Two defects are obvious in the adjustment which the people of Nea Eleftherohori are making to their straitened circumstances. In the first place, there is no certainty that the boys pursuing a secondary school education will be able to find jobs when their training is completed. In 1956, there were three or four graduates of the gymnasium living in the village, waiting for something to turn up. One of them was working as a laborer on a road gang — a fate considered a terrible indignity to an educated man, even by his peasant relatives. But I was told that so far, "sooner or later," everyone who had finished the gymnasium course had been able to get a job in town, usually in the government civil service; and the parents who were sending their boys to school seemed to have no serious doubts that in due course their sons, too, might find a government desk to sit behind. If their hopes should be betrayed, then of course the whole campaign for maintaining family standards of living will be in danger of breaking down. Bitter disillusionment and discontent may then gain ground, especially among the educated young men. This is a real danger, for even a civil service as capacious as that of Greece cannot absorb indefinitely the gymnasium graduates of many villages like Nea Eleftherohori; and, of course, the gymnasium training does not prepare the boys for anything but white-collar work.

The second defect is psychological. Long postponement of marriage through the dowry represents a drastic alteration of older peasant customs. The dowry has always been a part of marriage customs in Greece, but it used to be relatively small and easily within the means of the average family. Moreover, not to marry off one's daughters at a rather early age — before twenty-two or so — was regarded as a disgrace. It was felt that something must be wrong, either with the girl or with her parents; that she was running a grave risk of immorality and consequent loss of reputation; and that the parents were delinquent in their duty if they failed to marry her off in the bloom of her youth. Because the new customs run contrary to these older attitudes, a very special tension exists among the farmers of Nea Eleftherohori. They feel it is wrong that their young people cannot marry when they should; they feel even more strongly that marriages must wait until the means of livelihood are assured. This requires the new dowry and land inheritance pattern. But no one is happy with the way the system has worked out, particularly the young people themselves, who see a long and dreary time of waiting ahead before they can hope to start families of their own.

This discontent is compounded by the feeling, which seems very strong in the village, that people in the towns have the best of everything: less work, more income; less boredom, more excitement. City standards of dress and manners have made extraordinary inroads in recent years, and aspiration toward a more comfortable and less laborious life is very strong.

Consequently, although by economic criteria the village is very much better off than before, and although the political tensions within the village have sunk back into insignificance, discontent is much alive and near the surface. It no longer takes political form as it did during and immediately after the war, when the Communists appealed to, and found a response among, many of the young people. As long as the majority of families in the village continue to see a path by which they may expect to maintain or modestly increase the standard of living they have enjoyed hitherto, it is likely that discontent will remain personal and private. As yet, hard work, saving and waiting seem to promise a solution; and with such hope present discontents seem bearable. But if some day the hopes turn out to have been in vain, then one may expect to see an active movement of political dissent and revolt appear in Nea Eleftherohori once more.

As compared with Lofiscos, therefore, Nea Eleftherohori is a good deal farther along the path toward a new social and psychological adjustment of village life. The less spacious economic base from which Nea Eleftherohori started compelled an earlier and more energetic adoption of new agricultural techniques; the old-fashioned frame in which the peasant family and community flourished from time immemorial has largely been transformed or discarded; and city standards have come in, not so much in fact as in aspiration.

PALEO CORINTHOS

Paleo Corinthos, or Old Corinth, stands on the site of the ancient city, on the isthmus between the Corinthian and Saronic gulfs. The imposing mass of Acrocorinth, crowned by extensive and well-preserved Venetian fortifications, dominates the village, whereas the ruins from classical times are comparatively inconspicuous. The modern town of Corinth lies on the shore some five miles off, and has taken over the commercial functions once centered in the ancient city. Until very recently, Old Corinth remained the mere village it had been in Turkish times.

It is, however, a much larger village than either Lofiscos or Nea Eleftherohori. Its population was officially reckoned to be 1,530 in 1947; by 1956 the figure had grown to 1,850. This growth was only partly due to natural increase, for the village had acquired sixty "heads of family," mostly migrants from hill villages in the neighborhood, during the years between 1950 and 1956. Some of these immigrants brought families with them, others married into the village, but exact figures of the number of persons who have moved into the village are not available.

Nevertheless, Old Corinth definitely exhibits the pattern of internal migration which may in time allow the hillsmen of Greece to share in the rising prosperity of the villages of the plains, for migration into the community from the hills has been in part offset by another current of migration from Old Corinth into larger urban centers — either to nearby New Corinth or to Athens, some seventy miles off. Thirty-five to forty persons moved away to these centers between 1947 and 1956, according to the village president.

The reason for this mobility is that Old Corinth has become prosperous as never before. For centuries the agriculture of the community has centered upon currants; and since the seventeenth century the major market for this crop has been in England. Commercial agriculture is therefore no novelty, but the prosperity of the village has long been heavily at the mercy of the English market, and, more recently, access to this market has depended largely upon the Australian currant crop. To cultivate, pick, dry and sort currants is a labor-consuming task; and the Australian labor shortage in the postwar years proved a remarkable blessing for Corinth. Since 1954, when devaluation of the drachma cleared the way for export, currant prices have been good.

This is only a small part of Corinth's good fortune. Owing largely to unusually wise and energetic leadership on the part of the village president, who has enjoyed a unique standing in the community, the two cooperatives which were organized before the war and were bankrupted during it were re-established by 1952. Through their instrumentality a series of important changes have come to the agriculture of the village. Fertilizer, bought through the cooperatives, has played its usual role in increasing wheat yields. In addition, a new variety of wheat has been introduced by the agricultural extension agent; this has still further increased the harvest, so that in 1956 the farmers counted on between 200 and 300 okes of wheat per stremma, compared with their prewar expectation of 80 to 100. The co-ops also have been able to buy two tractors and two harvesting machines that cultivate all the crop land of the community. These machines are hired out to neighboring villages when not needed in Old Corinth, and bring in a fair sum of money.

The most significant step, however, has been the drilling of irrigation wells. Irrigation began on a modest scale before the war, but in 1947 fuel for the pumping engines was hard to come by and many of the thirty wells the village then possessed were not used fully. By 1956 the number of wells and pumps had increased to 163, and all were in full use. Most of the suitable land in the village has come under irrigation. On this land, the villagers raise garden vegetables, especially tomatoes, and despatch them daily to the Athens market by truck. The result, in terms of money income, is spectacular. I was assured that a farm now yields ten times the income it supplied before the war.

Old Corinth has also benefited from the revival of tourism. In 1955, some 72,000 tourists visited the archaeological museum and the ruins on the outskirts of the village; and most of these visitors left at least some small change behind them in one of the coffee houses or in the new tourist restaurant which the government constructed in 1955. Moreover, Old Corinth lies near the new electric power line. Electricity came to the village for the first time in 1956. Of all the changes benefiting them in recent years, this was the one the villagers most praised, perhaps because it was the newest.

Very considerable inequalities in landholding exist within the village. As a result, some families have profited far more than others from the new prosperity. Since the Greek War of Independence (1821–30), if not before, landholdings in Old Corinth have not been disturbed by wholesale government action, of the sort characteristic in the northern part of the country. The processes of inheritance and marriage settlements, supplemented by purchase and sale of land — something almost unheard of in the northern villages — have resulted in the establishment of extremely complicated property relationships. Renting and sharecropping are both common. In addition, many fields are subject to concurrent rights held by several individuals. This situation arises when heirs have refrained from subdividing an inheritance because such division would reduce the fields to absurdly small dimensions. Instead it has long been the custom to cultivate such fields as a unit and to divide the proceeds, according to some agreed proportion, among all those who have a claim thereto. Over the generations, such concurrent rights have sometimes ramified widely; but the complications of remote family and property relationships are something Greek peasant farmers are able to keep very clear in their heads, with or without written documents.

A substantial proportion of the inhabitants of Old Corinth possess no land at all. They make a living by working for others, either for day wages or on a sharecropping basis. With the introduction of tomatoes and other vegetable crops, together with the revival of the currant market, a definite, though seasonal, shortage of labor has appeared. Substantial farmers (that is, men owning 10 to 20 acres of land) complained of not being able to find enough hands to help them cultivate their fields, even though the wages they paid in the currant fields were higher than wages for unskilled labor in Athens. It is these wage rates, of course, that have attracted new settlers from the hills; but the fact that such labor is seasonal, lasting for only about four months in the year, means that families depending entirely on wage work are often in very hard straits.

The unparalleled prosperity that the years since 1953 have brought to the farmers of Corinth has been accompanied by the development of a number of nonagricultural occupations within the village. Several new stores and two new coffee houses have come into existence as well as the fancy restaurant for tourists. A number of persons also make a living as tourist guides. The richest men in the village, however, are merchants who have organized the delivery of tomatoes and other vegetables to the Athens market; they employ truck drivers, not all of whom live in the village. The two cooperatives employ, between them, a full-time, professionally trained secretary. The museum has a small staff of caretakers and curators. The village school had 210 pupils in 1956 and employed three teachers. A priest officiates in a handsome new church, which the villagers have built out of their own resources. Old Corinth, in other words, is developing into a small town, and ceasing to be a mere village. If the plan, only talked about in 1956, for establishing a small canning factory to preserve tomatoes is ever realized, the transition to a town status will become definite.

Nevertheless, from one point of view, the community has so far remained thoroughly traditional in its social organization. The substantial farmers of Old Corinth continue to adhere to age-old patterns of family life. When it comes time for their children to marry, the daughters are dowered, partly with money and partly with a share of crop land, vineyard and olive grove; and sons, similarly, inherit their portion of the parental farm. Clearly, if there are more than two children — and this is almost universally the case — the new generation will have to face life on a smaller piece of land; but this problem does not seem especially acute to the larger farmers. An interesting indicator of this fact is that in 1956 only thirty boys from the village attended the gymnasium in New Corinth close by — a smaller number than Nea Eleftherohori was sending to a considerably more distant school, though the population of Old Corinth is nearly three times as great as that of the Macedonian village. As a matter of fact, the recent increases in the yield from Old Corinth's land have been so great that a new family can face life with equanimity, even owning only half as much land as their parents possessed.

For the landless segment of the population, and for those who own only a tiny plot insufficient to maintain a family anyway, the problem is quite different. Here the major consideration is not land but wages; and as long as there is work, and wages are comparatively good, the new generation can start off with little or nothing but a strong back and willing hands, and hope to make out about as well as their fathers have done. For them also, there is no overwhelming pressure to postpone marriage in order to keep up a standard of living.

As a result, the population statistics of Old Corinth do not show nearly so drastic a change from the prewar years as is evident in Nea Eleftherohori. Yet the birth rate has dropped in Old Corinth also. In the 1930's (when the population of the village was, of course, a good deal smaller) recorded births ranged between 58 and 46 each year. Since 1947 the range has been from 46 to 33. This change, however, has been nearly offset by a parallel drop in the death rate. Before the war, deaths averaged close to 30 each year; since 1947 the average has been a little over 12. The drop has mainly been due to the elimination of malaria through DDT; whereas Old Corinth was formerly one of the many places in Greece badly afflicted by that disease, there was no malaria in 1956.

Particularly fortunate conditions in Old Corinth — tourism, irrigation, the proximity to the Athens market, and the effective leadership of the village president — have permitted the villagers to maintain their old family customs almost unchanged, and in spite of the rapid growth of population which such customs entail, they have not had to sacrifice their standard of living. Instead, living conditions have improved, with electricity, tractors and the like.

This is a situation very rare in Greece. It makes Old Corinth the happiest village I visited, a community at peace with itself and with the world, mildly surprised by the prosperity that has descended upon it, and generally well content with the way things are going. The contrast is strong with the internal condition of the village in 1947, when, like Nea Eleftherohori, the community was sharply divided between left and right. In 1947, indeed, the bitterness between the two political parties was far deeper than in Nea Eleftherohori, for in Old Corinth the political lines were drawn, more or less exactly, between farmers and landless men, that is, between buyers and sellers of labor. Two particularly squalid "political" murders occurred within the village in the last days of the German occupation; and the Communist-inspired regime, which lasted for a few months in 1944, aroused strong revulsion among the substantial farmers. These memories now seem almost forgotten, though the sense of solidarity between rich and poor in Old Corinth is by no means so strong as the community feeling among the villagers of Nea Eleftherohori, where everybody is nearly equal economically.

The inequalities in landholding, and the existence of a fairly numerous landless class in the village, certainly constitute a potential source of trouble. If currant and tomato prices should fall, or if more migrants from the hills should come to the village and push wages down by competing for jobs in the fields, the existing harmony and general satisfaction could easily break down. The more elaborate social stratification and intricate economic integration which the development from simple village into small town involves carries with it a special vulnerability: vulnerability to fluctuations in distant markets, and vulnerability to social stresses within the community itself. This is perhaps the price Old Corinth has to pay for its remarkable economic progress in recent years.

This progress may remind us that there is another sense in which the social structure of Old Corinth shows itself far more flexible and hospitable to innovation than the other villages described. For while family and marriage customs have not undergone important modification, the occupational patterns of the community have shown important changes; and in at least one instance a landless and once very poor man has risen to a position of wealth and importance by becoming a successful merchant. Old Corinth has given far more scope to individual and cooperative enterprise than either Lofiscos or Nea Eleftherohori. Yet this development, too, is in line with old Greek tradition. The self-made man, particularly the self-made merchant or storekeeper, rising to wealth and respectability by virtue of his mother wit and shrewdness in buying and selling, has been a prominent figure in Greek society for at least two centuries; and it has always been the marginal man in the village social hierarchy — the man who has had no land to keep him busy — who has naturally gravitated to such occupations when opportunity has opened. Innovation in Old Corinth has thus taken traditional forms.

Since 1912, rural Greece has been fundamentally divided between villages like Old Corinth, which can look back to generations of substantially undisturbed evolution, and those villages where within recent memory radical governmental intervention entirely transformed earlier landholding patterns. The division is geographical. In Old Greece, meaning Greece within the boundaries that existed before 1881, village life has not suffered drastic upheaval since 1821, if then. Changes have come slowly and by evolution. The case is far otherwise in New Greece — Thessaly, Macedonia, Epirus and Thrace. There the violent elimination of Turkish landlords and peasants through war was followed by governmental creation of egalitarian peasant communities. This amounted to an agrarian revolution from above, in some cases fully satisfying the peasants — as in Lofiscos — but often failing to do so, as in Nea Eleftherohori.

The slower evolution of village life in Old Greece has meant, at least until the present, the preservation of a fairly firm cake of custom, governing the daily lives of the inhabitants. In this respect, Old Corinth is quite typical. Consequently, in spite of the contrast between rich peasant and landless laborer, the social stratification within these peasant communities has not bred so many revolutionists as have been bred by the hardships of life in an equality of poverty, characteristic of many villages in the north. Conservatism, royalism, traditionalism have all centered in the south; while radicalism, republicanism, restlessness and revolution have found their strongest expression in the north.

Yet while these generalizations are true, I must hasten to add that the villages of the plains never were the main centers of political revolt. Too many had too much to lose in such communities. Rather it was in the hill villages, where life was harder and the prospect of maintaining a given standard of life was dimmer, that revolution found its most congenial ground. Since the latter part of the eighteenth century, if not before, this has been the really vulnerable point in Greek society, the source of major disturbance and of recurrent civil violence. In the hills, even more than in the plains, the future stability or instability of Greek society is likely to be decided in time to come, as it has in times past. Let us therefore leave the plains and turn to the hills.

Hill Villages

KOTTA

Kotta is situated in the far northwestern corner of Greece, about five miles from the Albanian border, and not more than fifteen miles from the point where Yugoslavia, Albania and Greece adjoin. Flowing past the village is a small stream which in due course descends to join the Aliakmon River. The valley slopes are steep, and the villagers possess only 500 stremmata (125 acres) of arable soil. Much of this is thin patches on the hillsides; of good bottom land the community has less than ten acres.

When I visited the village in 1947, the inhabitants were starving. Seemingly innumerable children peeped out from every house, many of them showing bloated bellies beneath motley rags that served as clothing but scarcely covered their nakedness. The village was then in the hands of the guerrillas, who had stationed a detachment of fifteen boys (the eldest was not more than eighteen) in the community. The ordinary speech was Slavic, and at least some of the villagers felt that it would be better for them if their village belonged to Yugoslav Macedonia. Macedonian national feeling may have played some part in this attitude, but probably the major determinant was the knowledge that conditions across the border were not quite so hard as those they faced in Greece.

The people of Kotta were, indeed, living under war conditions. The Greek army had blocked the main road between Florina and Kastoria, which runs not far from the village site, and no vehicles could pass without special permits; men could still get through on foot by taking off across open country, but there was little incentive to do so. Work could not be found down in the plains, and a man from Kotta, with the trace of a Slavic accent in his Greek, was courting arrest or a beating if he ventured into territory controlled by the Greek army or police. Resentment against the Greek authorities was widespread, although one man in the village, in speaking to me privately, made it clear that he at least did not like to contribute to the upkeep of the guerrilla garrison that controlled the village.

The population of the village was 630 persons, of whom over 200 were under fifteen years of age. Thus there was about one fifth of an acre of agricultural land per head, land that was miserably poor to begin with. Clearly the village could not live on its agriculture; and even when it had been safe to graze sheep on the barren mountain slopes, as it was not in 1947, the village still could not begin to maintain itself on local resources. The villagers calculated that they could produce food for about four months in the year; the deficit had to be made good outside.

In prewar years two means had been found to make ends meet. The men of the village were accomplished masons, and traveled far and wide over Greece seeking work as builders. In addition, they found work in various sorts of heavy construction — road building, irrigation works and the like. But in 1947 such jobs were not to be had, at least not by men with a Slavic accent.

The second, and perhaps more important, resource was remittances from abroad. The village had begun to send men overseas, mainly to Canada and Australia, even before the first world war. During the interwar years, the migration had continued despite growing barriers to free movement. In Toronto, Canada, and in Sydney, Australia, natives of Kotta had founded regular little colonies, and the members of these emigrant groups, all of whom were related to one another in some degree, helped to finance the continued emigration. Each family expected to send at least one son overseas, and that son was in turn expected to send back enough of his earnings to keep his parents fed and clothed, and to help out his brothers and sisters who stayed home. When the Greek army interrupted communication with the outside world this vital supply of cash was cut off. In 1947, therefore, the villagers were trying to spread out four months' food over the twelve months of the year.

Their diet was cornbread and little else. Nearly all of their sheep, whose milk had once helped to correct the deficiencies of a maize diet, had been slaughtered during the occupation; and the prevalence of skin diseases and a certain lassitude in their movements clearly indicated that malnutrition was added to undernourishment. They missed salt more acutely than anything else. There had been none in the village for several weeks when I was there.

Kotta remained in guerrilla hands until August 1949. It was luckier than some of its neighboring communities inasmuch as there was no fighting in the immediate environs, so that the houses of the village escaped without more than casual damage. But the villagers could not escape from famine, nor from disease that naturally followed in the wake of prolonged and drastic undernourishment. When I returned in 1956, the population of the village had shrunk to 188, less than one third of what it had been in 1947. The average number of persons per family had declined to 2.4, whereas in 1947 families with fewer than three children were a rarity and five or six children per family was closer to the average.

About one hundred of the former inhabitants of the village were simply missing. They had gone off, in desperation, looking for food or safety and had not come back. Most, presumably, had died or been killed. In addition, the village priest said that about fifty of the village men were known to have been killed while serving with the guerrillas; and five families had moved west across the Albanian frontier in 1949 when the guerrilla retreat took place. But the largest single factor in the decline of population was the removal of the village children by the guerrillas. A total of 225 children, between the ages of two and twelve, had been taken north in the early stages of the war, and only three had returned. A few letters had come from some of them, originating in places as remote as Turkestan, Poland and Czechoslovakia; but most had not been heard from, and no one in the village knew whether they were alive or dead.

The evacuation of the village children may well have been conceived by the guerrilla authorities as a humanitarian measure. Considering the state of the village as I saw it in 1947, such an interpretation seems quite plausible. This was not the way the bereft parents viewed the matter, however. They gave no very coherent explanation of why the children were taken, but the abduction was remembered in 1956 as the greatest crime the guerrillas committed. Not a few parents have been left childless, and this, by traditional village standards, is a bitter disaster. Who will look after them in their old age?

Still another factor in the drastic depopulation of Kotta has been emigration. As soon as communications with the outside world became possible again, relatives rallied round in Toronto and Sydney, and helped a total of fifty-six persons to emigrate. The process is still going on. When I visited the village in 1956, a young man and his mother were on the verge of departure for Australia, where they would join cousins who were financing the voyage.

Yet in spite of the sorrows which have visited every family in the village, and in spite of the terrible suffering all have been through, the spirit of the village in 1956 seemed amazingly relaxed and calm — almost happy. The survivors gave the impression of being profoundly surprised to find themselves still alive. But what is more important, everyone now has enough to eat. The village land can feed the population; there is now no need to look for work outside; and remittances from abroad permit some families to indulge in small luxuries — kerosene lamps, for example. I even saw two fine Swiss watches on the wrists of young men dressed in homespun.

In the immediate postwar period, Kotta benefited somewhat from government help. The villagers were given glass to repair the windows of their houses, and some lumber for doors and window frames, so that their houses are in better repair today than in 1947. In 1954 a stout stone bridge was built across the stream with government funds, and the villagers made a rude road to connect Kotta with the outside world. Vehicles can therefore come into the village, though few come, since the villagers have little need of anything from beyond their own small valley.

Their agriculture is much the same as before, with corn almost the sole crop. The village flock of sheep is slowly growing back to prewar proportions, thanks in part to the government's having given each family four sheep as a start. The village also has a few cattle — another government gift — which not only yield milk but are harnessed to the plows as well. All this represents a return to familiar patterns.

The only agricultural innovation that has so far come to Kotta is the experimental sowing of alfalfa on one of the good acres of bottom land. This measure was recommended to the village by a government extension agent in the hope of remedying one of the crying weaknesses of its traditional economy — the lack of winter fodder for animals. Leaves cut from trees and dried cornstalks have been normal winter fare for cattle and sheep; and since the village stands more than two thousand feet above sea level, the winter is both long and severe. As a result the animals emerge thin and weak from the winter months. Yet the villagers are not altogether convinced that the new crop is worth while. Alfalfa was planted for the first time in 1955, and while it did help to feed the cattle, the new crop occupied one of the best pieces of bottom land the village possesses, where corn for human food grows better than in almost any other spot. To replace human with animal food on such land is a considerable sacrifice — too much of a sacrifice if the population of the village should once again begin to grow.

As things are today, the villagers lead a very leisurely life. Work in the fields takes at most three months of the year. There is no need of outside work, and no one attempts to find it. For nine months of the year, consequently, the men have plenty of time on their hands. They use it in sitting around the village and talking. Their talk is easy and friendly. Men who fought on opposite sides in the guerrilla war could joke about it without any trace of bitterness. As a matter of fact, many of the survivors had fought on both sides, first with the guerrillas and then with the Greek army. Those who stayed with the guerrillas were killed, or else disappeared into Albania. Except for the loss of their children, there seems no inclination to blame the guerrillas for what happened; nor is there any perceptible hostility against the Greek government. The general feeling about the war is that it was all an absurd nightmare in which the villagers themselves were no more than victims, rather than participants. As Slavs, the villagers cannot easily share Greek nationalism, and Communist ideas and ideals seem to have left no impression upon them. Presumably, the few who took those ideas seriously departed with the retreating guerrilla army. For those who remain, the vision of Sydney or Toronto means far more than any ideological paradise.

One of the most surprising changes in Kotta is the prevalence of Greek as the normal and natural speech, for communication among the villagers themselves as well as with strangers. "We are all Greek now," one of the young men said, and explained that both in the guerrilla and in the regular army, the language and sentiment had been Greek. Only the old people of the village speak Slav any more, he said. Even more to the point, the villagers know that they are now much better off than the people in Yugoslav Macedonia, with whom they so recently felt a degree of kinship.

Since 1954 no representative of the Greek government has lived in the village. An army detachment, which had been there from 1949, departed in 1954, leaving patriotic slogans on the walls of the buildings used as barracks. No gendarmes came to replace the soldiers. Hence the village has been left very largely to its own devices. The inhabitants like it that way. As is true of all villages in Greece, the government no longer tries to collect direct taxes from Kotta (as it did before the war), but contents itself with a 2 per cent sales tax on products sold in town markets. This, for Kotta, amounts to paying almost no taxes at all, for the inhabitants sell almost nothing. This, too, pleases the villagers.

Kotta, therefore, is a community in which thoroughly old-fashioned attitudes prevail. In spite of the harrowing guerrilla war — or rather because of it — life has resumed its old, familiar channels; and since everyone now has enough to eat without having to venture into the outside world, the villagers seem well content to settle down within their nearly self-sufficient valley and let the world go by.

The real question for the future is whether or not the village will proceed once again to breed children on the reckless scale that prevailed before. The age structure of the surviving population is altogether anomalous, the removal of all children between the ages of two and fourteen in 1948 having left a great gap. Moreover, military losses and emigration overseas mainly affected young men and women of the next older age groups. The potentially childbearing population has therefore been drastically depleted, so much so that out of a total of seventy-seven families in 1956, the village contained only four or five couples of childbearing age. (One must bear in mind that in a community where very early marriages have been the rule, a woman of thirty or thirty-five is already old.) Between 1952 and 1956 there were only four marriages in the village, twelve births, sixteen deaths. Under the circumstances, it seems certain that the population will decrease still further in the immediate future.

Yet even four or five families could turn out to be quite enough to repopulate the village, if the old patterns of early marriage and numerous children prevail. Indeed, the close blood relationships of all the villagers suggests that in times past the community may well have contained only a handful of families from whom hundreds (or, counting those overseas, thousands) in due course descended. Thanks to the depopulation brought by the guerrilla war, the traditional life of Kotta has become easy once again, and if the young people accept the old ways, and do not allow the glitter of urban life overseas, reflected in the letters and money orders sent back by friends and relatives, to change their outlook, then it seems fairly certain that within a decade or less the depopulation of the village will come to a halt, and rapid growth in numbers will begin once more. If so, after something like thirty or forty years Kotta will probably be back in the impossible position of 1947.

This cycle is, I believe, the key to much Balkan history. The peasant family system was adjusted, from age-old antiquity, to supply large numbers of children, most of whom died from violence or disease before attaining adulthood. With the more or less effective pacification of the countryside in the last couple of centuries, together with the elimination of some epidemic diseases and the control of others, this age-old balance was thrown out of kilter, so that the peasant population began (as early as the mid-eighteenth century) to run far ahead of the development of resources that might sustain it.

In politics, the result was a series of risings against the lords of the plains, which centered in the marginal hill villages. Until 1912, the lords of the Macedonian plains were of course Turks, and Greek nationalism (like other Balkan nationalisms) was therefore able with perfect propriety to combine territorial expansion with social revolution, and pit hill against plain in the name of individual freedom and national self-determination. The first clear example of this phenomenon was the Greek War of Independence of 1821–30. The long series of revolts and irregular wars of the nineteenth century in the European dominions of the Ottoman Empire continued the process; and the guerrilla movements in Yugoslavia, Albania and Greece during (and in Greece after) the second world war were only its latest manifestations. In this most recent period, however, the lords of the plains were not Turks any longer, and were not even landlords. Instead they were fellow peasants and co-nationals. The difference was cloaked during World War II by the fact that Germans and Italians were in the plains, and to attack them served to justify the far more genuine assault upon the plains villages — from which, after all, the major food supply of the guerrilla forces had to come. Only in Greece, between 1946 and 1949, did the divergence between nationalism and social revolution become clear; and even in that instance, as pointed out above, most guerrillas felt themselves to be Greek patriots as well.

Kotta's wartime experience shows dramatically how such warfare brought its own solution to the problem of overpopulation — cruel, blind, bloody, but effective. Depopulation, such as Kotta suffered, certainly sufficed to solve for a generation or so the problem of too many mouths and not enough land. When the crisis passed, survivors could settle back to a more or less satisfactory life again, until their growing numbers should once more make the traditional style of life impossible within the limits of the hill valleys. In times past, Balkan hillsmen then had to seek sustenance from the plains, either by peaceful labor or by armed forays.

As far as Kotta and villages like it are concerned, it now seems to me an open question whether the old cycle will repeat itself again or whether new standards of expectation and conduct will make sufficient inroads upon the traditional peasant family system to check early marriage and rapid multiplication of numbers. Through overseas emigration, the modern city has made its mark on Kotta. All but a few young people want to leave, and many have done so. At the same time, the handful who remain appear to be conforming to the old ways. Perhaps the critical turn will come as their children grow up; for if the rising generation elects to look beyond the confines of the village — and if the possibilities of migration, either within Greece or overseas, exist — then, perhaps, as the population of the village begins to press once again upon the limits of local production, the young people may decline to continue the old, economically suicidal pattern, and will instead seek their fortunes far afield, and refuse to marry into hopeless poverty at home. It depends more than anything else, perhaps, upon the degree of communication that may come to exist between the outside world and the villagers. In 1956 these contacts were limited. Newspapers came seldom; vehicles rarely. But the village did possess a radio that brought daily news from Athens; and emigrants' letters were perhaps the most important of all the channels of contact with the great world beyond the valley in which Kotta nestles.

Survivors of the older generation — those who have lost their children to the guerrillas — seem to have no doubts or reservations in wishing to see more and more children about again. The priest complained of how empty and joyless the village was without the throngs of children he knew before. He deeply regretted the loss of five of his own whom the guerrillas had taken. Yet he was fortunate in having one child still with him, a girl who was too young to leave her mother when the guerrillas took the older children. As for the attitudes of the younger generation in the village, I could not satisfy myself. In the presence of their elders, they generally kept quiet, and certainly refrained from any overt dissent. Whether they, too, shared the traditional view that the more children one has the better off one is (assured thereby of God's blessing and of sustenance in old age), I could not tell.

CHERASIA

Cherasia is a village in Thessaly near the base of Mount Pelion, some six air miles from Volos, the fourth city of Greece. Along the winding road, however, it lies about twelve miles from Volos; and before 1952 the only road connection with the village required a detour of about twenty-four miles around the mountain. The community is an old one. Local tradition holds that it was founded 680 years ago. Until the Germans destroyed the "upper" village in 1943, the community led a semi-migratory life, spending the summer months high up the mountain where a natural spring supplied water, and coming down to the foot of the mountain only in winter, when the flocks could pasture on the stubble of other villages' grain fields. The villagers looked upon the upper village as their real home, the lower one as only a temporary shelter.

The traditional occupations of the village were sheepherding and charcoal burning. Once upon a time, sixty or seventy years ago, the main support of the community may well have been sheep, pastured on the rough mountain in summer, and on grain stubble in the winter. Then, by degrees, charcoal burning and woodcutting became more important. Two factors presumably led to this change. One was the rise of Volos as an important urban center, requiring charcoal as fuel for cooking and for heating houses. To supply the rising demand, the villagers of Cherasia began cutting off the forests of Mount Pelion with a new energy. A second factor was the growth of population in Cherasia itself. As more families appeared, sheep could not support them all, because the pastures could not be readily extended. So the people fell back on exploitation of the forests.

This "ancient" history is mostly speculation. I was not able to get any clear account of their distant past from the men of the village. What they did know was that in 1905 three families had secured title to 100 stremmata (25 acres) of land apiece in the little valley that spreads out below the site of their winter quarters at the foot of the mountain. At that time, very likely, the free villagers of the mountain saw little or no attraction in the toilsome life of a farmer, and preferred to keep to their ancient shepherd's way of life, supplemented by woodcutting and charcoal burning.

About the time of the first world war, things changed. As the population continued to grow, sheep and charcoal no longer sufficed to provide a satisfactory living for the members of the community. Many of them began to clear little patches of rocky mountainside in the hope of raising a crop or two on the land. Their tenure was legally recognized by a governmental survey made in 1922, which assigned to each family title to the patches its members had cleared and cultivated in preceding years. During the interwar period the pressure to find supplementary means of livelihood through agriculture continued to mount. In 1938, village authorities parceled out 500 stremmata of what had been common pasture to private family ownership. No further property changes had occurred in the village up to 1956.

The brute fact remains, however, that fields cleared from mountain slopes are miserable agricultural land. These produce a crop of only about 30 okes of wheat per stremma (a little more than 4 bushels per acre), and are capable of doing that only for two or three years, after which time the field has to be abandoned for a while until its dubious fertility has been restored. The president of the village told me that he allows the villagers to clear land wherever they can find anything that seems worth clearing, even though this goes beyond the letter of the law and encroaches on what is properly common pasture.

The desperate effort to find more cultivable land throughout the interwar, wartime and postwar years reflects the growing exhaustion of the forests, upon which the majority of the village population have come to depend. The villagers have cut off the trees farther and farther up the mountain, until only a little scrub oak remains; and even this is so thin that a man has to work hard and long to collect enough wood to make a charcoal burning. Since World War II, indeed, it has become more usual to sell the wood in its raw form, even though this multiplies transport problems, and means far less money per donkey-load delivered to Volos.

Within the village itself bitter feelings began to rise during the interwar period. The three families that had turned to agriculture in 1905, thus securing possession of the only decent agricultural land in the whole village, were able to keep their farms together. In 1956, one of the three families had removed entirely to Volos, and was renting out its land on a sharecropping basis to poorer families in the village. The other two "rich" families (who by any standard other than that of Cherasia were still poor) were each represented in the village by a single household, presumably because other descendants of the original owners had left for town. The result was a striking economic contrast between the poor woodcutters, whose painfully cleared hillside patches were scarcely worth the labor of cultivation, and the "rich" families. Indeed, the members of the two village households owning 100 stremmata each did not find it necessary to work the land themselves. Like the absentee in Volos, they also rented their fields on a sharecropping basis to the others. The president of the village in 1956 was the head of one of these households; he had let the nail of his little finger on one hand grow in order to prove to everyone that he was exempt from manual labor. He was also the only fat man I saw in the village.

The bad feeling in Cherasia was not simply a matter of economics, however. Shepherds have had a proud tradition in Greece. Heavy manual labor is beneath them, and they have always felt themselves superior to the grubbing farmers of the plains. Moreover, a tradition of violence has always lain near the surface among shepherds. In days not so very far past, it was part of the shepherd's job to protect his flock from wolves. Even today a few wolves are said to survive in remote parts of Greece; and whenever public order breaks down, far more dangerous two-footed wolves, armed with guns, quickly appear. The transition from shepherd to bandit has always been easy. A shepherd losing his flock must almost automatically become a two-footed wolf himself, preying on other shepherds or, better yet, on the fat, stolid landlords and peasants of the plain.

In view of these traditions, one can better understand the spirit of Cherasia. Free shepherds, traditionally ready for violence, were being ground down to a status beneath that of the weaklings who in 1905 had preferred the indignity of labor to the leisure of mountain pastures; and to the people of Cherasia this seemed a clear reversal of the proper social order. They were most unwilling to accept such a reversal. They were not farmers, and did not wish to become farmers. As a result, they did not do all they might have done to make their hillside agriculture rewarding. Field labor was, for them, a regrettable necessity, not a satisfying way of life. They made no effort at terracing, attempted no planting of fruit trees or of vines, and in general refused to borrow any of the traditional and very effective methods of Greek Mediterranean agriculture, even though there are villages on the other side of Mount Pelion, within less than two hours' walking distance, where these methods have been in use for centuries on land intrinsically no better than that of the Cherasia hillsides. (There is one important difference, however: because Cherasia's land faces north, toward the open Thessalian plain, cold winter winds blow across it and make olive cultivation impossible. But olive cultivation is and has always been the backbone of Mediterranean hillside agriculture. This undoubtedly is the reason why settlers from over the mountain never tried to exploit Cherasia's hillsides, leaving them to shepherds for winter pasture.)

The upshot of the history and traditions of Cherasia was that even before World War II, a thoroughly revolutionary mood prevailed in the village. The poor — which is to say nearly everybody in the village except the three families — felt the need to find a scapegoat for what was happening to them. They despised but also envied the three "rich" families, and felt that it would no more than serve them right to be plundered of all they had gained. The villagers also held the government and all other persons in authority vaguely responsible for the straits in which they found themselves. They could not help casting greedy eyes upon rich villages like Lofiscos, which lies within sight of Cherasia, a scant twenty miles across the flat Thessalian plain. But unlike most Greek villagers, they did not really want agricultural land; plunder was more in line with the tradition of the community.

The Communist-led guerrilla movement of World War II therefore found unusually ready and unanimous support in Cherasia. No one was willing to tell me how many men from the village joined the resistance during the occupation period; but my guess is that practically every able-bodied man took part at some time or other in guerrilla actions, even though some of the villagers remained ostensibly civilian. A consequence was that in 1943 a German expedition burnt all the houses of the upper village and made it uninhabitable. The people of Cherasia, fortunately, saw them coming and had time to escape over the mountain.

The "liberation" of Greece in 1944 brought no liberation to Cherasia. Quite the contrary, it interfered with the process by which armed men from the village had been able during the occupation to get grain and other goods from the plains. Consequently, when three men appeared on Mount Pelion in 1946 and summoned the young men of the village to take arms again, the response was immediate. When I visited the village in 1947, a guerrilla band, some thirty strong, was encamped in the ruins of the upper village. A detachment descended each evening to gather supplies from the inhabitants of the lower village and from other villages out in the plain. Most of the members of the band were sons of families living in lower Cherasia, although the leaders of the band came from elsewhere.

During the day, the Greek army, from a strong point in a neighboring plains village, took possession of Cherasia. Each morning a patrol of soldiers came to the village and demanded to know who had been collaborating with the guerrillas; each evening the guerrillas came down from the mountain and demanded to know who had been helping the soldiers. Under the circumstances, life was difficult, to say the least. The army sometimes beat those suspected of sympathizing with the guerrillas. In addition, irregular rightist bands visited the community several times and indulged in greater violence, killing several people and burning down seven houses. The guerrillas, too, burned some houses, including those belonging to the three "rich" families of the community. These had fled to Volos, together with some other families from the village. The people who remained were inclined to support the guerrillas.

About two weeks after my visit in 1947, the army evacuated all the remaining inhabitants of Cherasia to Volos. There they remained in refugee quarters for two and a half years. The last guerrilla band disappeared from Mount Pelion only in 1950, some six months after the main guerrilla army in the north had retreated across the Albanian frontier. It was therefore late in 1950 before the inhabitants of Cherasia were allowed — or compelled — to return to their village.

Government authorities were, however, well aware of the difficulties that confronted the community. The returned refugees were given every help to re-establish themselves. They received, gratis, 238 sheep to serve as a nucleus for their flock, as well as materials for the reconstruction of their houses, most of which had suffered damage. Officials issued seed and implements as well. A comprehensive work relief program was set up; for about two years after their return, the men of Cherasia received wages for working on projects that directly benefited their community. In this fashion the new road over the mountain was built — shortening the way to Volos by nearly half. Similarly, new and very handsome school and church buildings were constructed; and pipes from the spring in the upper village brought fresh water into lower Cherasia for the first time. This was vital if the population was to remain in the lower village the year around, since water had previously been unavailable there in summer. Another side of the government policy was to give no help toward reconstruction of the village of upper Cherasia — perched, as it was, high on the mountain beyond the reach of roads. No doubt the authorities in this fashion hoped to tie the villagers to the accessible lower village, and

thus prevent, or at least make more difficult, any future guerrilla action based upon the upper village.

The result of these expenditures is clearly visible today. The
village looks handsomer than ever before; the sound of flowing
water resounds refreshingly beside the neatly paved square in
the center of the village, and the bright new tile roofs of the
village shine in the sun. Only the houses of Nea Eleftherohori
rival the impressive outward appearance of Cherasia, and the
public structures of Nea Eleftherohori are far inferior to the
new ones of the Thessalian village.

Nor have governmental efforts ended there. An agricultural
extension agent visits Cherasia once or twice a month — a far
more frequent visitation than I found in any other village. He
attempted to establish viticulture and fruit trees in the village;
but the vines perished, and the fruit trees are still spindly sap-
lings, not yet bearing anything. Finally, additional water works
are in process of construction, on the strength of a loan from the
Ministry of Interior, issued free of interest and repayable in in-
stallments, starting only after five years. When this is finished,
there will be enough water to irrigate 50 stremmata (12½ acres)
of bottom land, and thus open up a new range of agricultural
possibilities for the village.

Certainly, no one can say that either money or skill has been
stinted in trying to make the life of Cherasia tolerable for its
inhabitants. Yet it was perfectly apparent in 1956 that the effort
had been totally inadequate. The people of the village were
sullen and suspicious, and felt no gratitude toward the government authorities who had done so much for them. The spirit of
the village seemed almost the same as in 1947, with the difference that now the rightists were again on top, and the majority
saw little hope for gaining even the nighttime control their
party had enjoyed in 1947. In talking with one or two of the villagers I gained the impression that they perversely hoped the

various government plans would fail. Indeed, I suspect that the vines which the agricultural extension agent planted so hopefully may have died, not because his plans were faulty, but because the villagers failed to look after them.

Aside from the fact that Communist sympathies were deeply implanted in the village even before the war and were strengthened during and after it by the guerrilla movement, one can point to two facts that help to explain the village attitude. First, the persons who stand to benefit principally from agricultural improvements are naturally those who possess good land — the three families that acquired the bottom land in 1905. For the others, on their miserable hillside patches, there is little the agricultural extension agent can do.

Second, and much more important, is the fact that in 1954 the government cracked down on woodcutting. Roughly half of the mountain slopes, which had been "theirs" for as long as the men of the village could remember, were set aside as a forest preserve where woodcutting was forbidden. The villagers did not stop cutting wood, but they now do it by stealth, mostly at night, and go out in parties, with watchmen posted in appropriate places to warn them when one of the forest guards comes by. Such activity smacks more than a little of warfare against constituted authority; and in proportion as the men of the village make their living in this illegal fashion, they maintain an open hostility against the government. In doing so they remain faithful to the old "freedom" of the village, characteristic of their shepherd forebears and of their guerrilla relatives and contemporaries.

Small wonder, therefore, that the villagers regard the government as hypocritical and inimical — pretending to give them something with one hand (but really giving mainly to the "rich" families) while with the other depriving them of their very livelihood. No theoretical arguments, to the effect that Greece badly needs reforestation, and that in the long run everyone, including the people of Cherasia, will benefit from re-establishment of real forests on Mount Pelion, carry any weight among the woodcutters who feel that their rights have been ruthlessly disregarded, and their traditional way of life endangered. They do not care to be farmers, and for all their ragged poverty, despise such slavish souls as are content to labor long and hard on the land.

A deep and painful irony lies in the fact that without the bureaucratic paternalism of the government most of the people of Cherasia would, in all probability, have died during the guerrilla war. What happened in Kotta, where the arm of the government did not reach, might well have happened also in Cherasia, if the inhabitants of the village had not been evacuated to Volos in 1947 and fed there — however miserably — for two and a half years by government relief. And if the population of the village had shrunk to one third of what it actually was in 1956, then it does not seem improbable that much of the present bitterness would have dissolved, because then something like the free traditional way of life would have been possible again. Governmental intervention between 1947 and 1950 prevented the operation of the brutal old-fashioned remedy for overpopulation; but governmental intervention since 1950 has not yet sufficed (and seems unlikely to suffice in the future) to provide a tolerable life for the population that has so successfully been preserved from famine, disease and violent death.

The official records of Cherasia were in considerable confusion in 1956, and I was not able to secure satisfactory figures on the present and past population of the village. The main reason for this state of affairs is that many families are registered as inhabitants of Cherasia, but do not reside there. When the villagers were sent back to their homes, everyone was supposed to go, and officially everyone did. Actually, about twenty-five families managed to escape official pressures and stayed in Volos, I was told, even though the records showed them back in the village. Similarly, a trickle of migration from the village into Volos since 1950 has gone unrecorded. With every sort of bureaucratic obstacle put in the way of legal transfer of residence from Cherasia to Volos, most of those who depart from the village simply neglect red tape and leave their names registered in Cherasia. They do so not by choice, since people officially registered as living in a village like Cherasia cannot claim unemployment benefits in Volos, and if they find no work, must either starve, rely upon relatives, or return to their village until better times offer a new start in town. This, of course, is the main reason why transfer of residence is made so difficult; the government could not afford to pay unemployment benefits to all the hungry men from the hills who might swarm into town if they could secure such payments.

Nevertheless, the villagers all agreed that more people were living in Cherasia in 1956 than had lived there before the war. A mean between conflicting estimates of the population came out close to 500 for 1956, and about 430 for 1940. The villagers reckon that their own local production supplies food for only two months in the year. The rest has to be bought with money earned by selling wood and charcoal, together with an occasional lamb from their flock.

Records of births and deaths were also in confusion, partly because children born in Volos to parents registered in Cherasia are supposed to be, but are not always in fact, entered in the village records. Partly, too, confusion arises from the custom of sending pregnant women to the Volos hospitals to give birth — a new departure in village custom, resulting from the wartime experience of living in the town, and facilitated by the existence of the new road. These children, too, sometimes escape the village registers, or are entered late. For what the figures may be worth, however, the records showed 45 births since 1951 as against 18 deaths, and everything I heard and observed in the village pointed to a very high rate of natural increase.

Marriages occur early. When nearly everyone lacks land that is worth much of anything, there is no tendency to wait until the new family can be assured a landed inheritance. One young man said, somewhat cynically: "What I had when I married was a donkey, an axe and a strong back. I still have all three, and three children as well." The donkey, I gathered, was his wife's contribution to the new household; the axe and the back, his own. This, it seems, is more or less normal in the village; and one can easily understand how a desire to escape the nagging poverty of the parental household would lead young men and girls into early marriage, in order at least to enjoy personal independence and the satisfactions of the marriage bed. Even though the rest of their traditional style of life seems on the verge of ruin, this still is possible. Feeling a general despair of ever being able to live decently, feeling also a certain reckless defiance of all forms of authority — including parental authority — there seems to persons such as the young man who spoke to me no reason not to marry as soon as one can find a partner.

In spite of the rebellious mood prevailing in Cherasia, the officials of the village in 1956, although supposedly elected, represented the extreme right. The president and secretary were both members of the "rich" families, possessing comparatively broad acres, and both were very emphatic and voluble in asserting that the only way to deal with Communists was to use force. Indeed, they said that peace could come to Cherasia and to Greece only when Russia was blown up by American atom bombs. How they were elected, I do not know, but I am certain the election was not a free one. Suspicion and thinly veiled hostility dominated the relation between the villagers and their official leaders.

Ten men in the village had come back after serving with the guerrillas, and were kept under informal surveillance. Some forty others had not returned, and most of these were presumed dead. Thirteen who had retreated behind the iron curtain in 1949 had, however, sent letters to their relatives. The village president, who provided these statistics, was obviously well informed on these matters and clearly believed that a major part of his duties was to keep a close watch upon leftists or suspected leftists.

Here, then, is a village scarcely better off than it was in 1947. In spite of the expenditure of tens of thousands of dollars, derived indirectly from American aid — indeed, *because* of such expenditure — the acute and untenable overcrowding of very poor land continues; and with it the political tensions of 1946–49 seethe, just beneath the surface. The only solution for Cherasia which seems to make any sense is to remove two thirds or more of the present population, and find land or work for them elsewhere. This has not been attempted; official policy has done just the opposite by placing barriers in the way of migration from the community.

Unfortunately, Volos, the natural outlet for the surplus population of Cherasia, was itself undergoing a first-class economic crisis in 1956. [4] The port, which is the economic heart of the

4. An earthquake which damaged many buildings in Volos rather badly in 1954 was, under the circumstances, a perverse blessing to many of the poorer families of the town. Repair and reconstruction got under way quickly, thanks to a special grant from the national budget (and assisted by a special American aid appropriation of $7 million for the purpose). This gave temporary work to many, but by 1956 this extraordinary source of employment had dwindled. At the same time, a large textile plant in the city went on part time, and discharged a large proportion of its working force, as a result of a general crisis in the Greek textile trade. Consequently, Volos was, like Cherasia, unusually clean and tidy in 1956, and unusually depressed.

city, was almost idle, so that serious unemployment was endemic in Volos, thus effectively blocking the easiest and most immediate escape for the hillsmen of Cherasia. In the Thessalian plain, villages like Lofiscos have not developed their agriculture to a level of intensity that would offer seasonal employment on a significant scale. Hence, for the time being the people of Cherasia are caught in a net scarcely of their own devising. At the same time they are stubbornly and angrily doing little or nothing to help themselves. It is not a hopeful situation, and if the general political climate of Greece should change, another guerrilla band could very likely be recruited from Cherasia without difficulty and at a moment's notice.

KARDAMILI

Kardamili lies on the sea, and can thus be described as a hill village only by looking inland, where high and barren hillsides rise abruptly from the coast, with only a small stream and a miniature delta to explain the location of the community. It is situated on the west coast of the central peninsula of the southern Peloponnese. Just to the south lies the wild and desolate country of Mani, a region where tribal organization and blood feud lasted into the twentieth century.

Kardamili raises a little wheat in the stream delta, but its major crop is olives. The rocky hillsides are covered with trees, skillfully planted in crevices and pockets of soil, many of which have been created artificially by terracing. The villagers reckon that they produce enough wheat to supply the community for about four months in the year; the rest has to be imported with money gained through the sale of olive oil.

Before the war, Kardamili added to its strictly agricultural resources by acting as a commercial center for a number of inland villages. They, too, exported olive oil, together with a few animals; and before roads were built, these villages brought their surplus on donkey-back (or on the hoof) to Kardamili, where it was put on board a small ship, and carried either to Athens or to Kalamata, the local metropolis, some thirty-five miles away on the rich Messenian plain. In addition, an oil-pressing plant was constructed in 1929 in Kardamili which employed as many as a hundred persons at the height of the season. Even when there were no olives to press, the plant kept open the year around by making soap and other products.

This was the basis upon which about 750 people were able to make a living in the village before the war. In recent years, however, the village has not prospered. The oil factory closed down permanently in 1940, depriving the village of what had been one of its most important resources. After the war, a new road, built in 1949–50, destroyed the importance of the port. Instead of bringing their olives to Kardamili on donkey-back and selling them there, the peasants of the hinterland loaded their produce directly onto trucks bound for Kalamata or Athens.

The new system was an obvious improvement on older methods of transport and marketing; but it meant that Kardamili, which for a few years between the wars had struggled toward becoming a miniature town, was compelled to sink back to a purely village status. One manifestation of this change is a decrease in population. In 1940, the village had about 750 inhabitants; in 1956 the population totaled only 512. War losses were insignificant, although guerrillas did kill two persons from the village. The whole community was forcibly evacuated to Kalamata in 1949 to prevent its exploitation by guerrilla bands that ranged even this far south. The evacuation was perhaps scarcely justified, however, since the guerrillas never again came near, and when the villagers returned in 1950 they found their houses intact.

They came back to a village whose earlier means of livelihood was being undermined by new roads. As this fact became
clear, emigration from the village commenced. Altogether,
something like two hundred persons left the village between
1950 and 1956. Only one family went overseas, to Australia. The
rest went either to Kalamata or to Athens. Among those who
have remained in the village, a considerable number have undertaken seasonal migration to the Messenian plain in order to
seek work with which to supplement the meager income from
their olive trees in the village. The biggest single source of employment which has opened up in recent years is work in rice
fields, developed in former salt marshes on the very edge of the
Messenian plain. For the villagers of Kardamili these fields in
Messenia have meant work and wages. Between eighty and
ninety persons, both men and women, leave the village each
year to help cultivate the rice fields. While working, they live
in shanties or even out of doors, and return to their homes in
Kardamili when work stops, or when something needs to be
done on their own land.

Within the village there are variations in wealth, but no family has so much land as to need to hire labor. Indeed, the village
secretary told me that the richest man in the village has only
forty days' work a year on his olive trees, while nearly one third
of all the village families own no land at all.

The only change that has come to the traditional agriculture
of the community is the introduction of fertilizer, but few families use it. A common opinion holds that fertilizer is bad for the
olive trees, and makes them short-lived by forcing an unnatural
proliferation of fruit. A more sophisticated farmer told me that
while the size of the fruit is increased by fertilizer, the quantity
of oil is not increased in anything like the same proportion and
its quality is lowered. Since the olive trees of this part of Greece
are famous for the high quality of the oil they produce, which

commands a premium price in Athens and elsewhere, the use of fertilizer becomes a somewhat dubious economic advantage.

The fact is, I believe, that the age-old adjustment of traditional peasant agriculture in the olive-growing regions of Greece is very nearly perfect. Certainly every scrap of potential soil is used in Kardamili, and the peasants know very well how to care for their trees. Except for chemical sprays that discourage a number of insect pests damaging to the crop, scientific agriculture has not yet devised any very important improvement upon traditional peasant methods of olive culture. But sprays were known in Kardamili before the war, and their use was resumed as soon as the chemicals became available.

In 1956 the village launched a project for bringing water down the mountain. An interest-free government loan made the enterprise possible; but, even when completed, the water pipes will not supply more than household needs, leaving a little over, perhaps, for watering gardens. Shortage of water has been the long-standing problem of the community. There was scarcely enough to drink when I was there, and each glassful was treated as something precious, since the women of the village had to carry it in jars from a trickling spring half a mile away.

Yet in spite of the stability of agricultural methods, the social system of the village, to all appearances, is beginning to change, more or less as the social system of Nea Eleftherohori is changing. For one thing, the villagers have begun to place great hopes in education, seeing in it a means of escaping from the land. Fifteen boys from the village were enrolled in the gymnasium in Kalamata in 1956, a quite considerable number in view of the fact that they had to live away from home, and thus had to meet expenses far greater than those confronting the boys from Nea Eleftherohori. In Kardamili itself, there is a school that teaches the first two years of the standard four-year gymnasium course. This school had eighty students, five more than were enrolled in the village primary school because boys from neighboring villages were in attendance. Within Kardamili, I was told, almost every boy goes through the first two years of gymnasium. Even without the final two years in Kalamata there is a chance, though not a good one, of finding a clerical job somewhere outside.

The other aspect of the adjustment characteristic of Nea Eleftherohori — postponement of marriage through the dowry system — is less advanced in Kardamili, but seems to be coming in. Dowries are rising, I was told, and even a man who owns no land himself may now ask a wife to bring him 2,000 okes of olive oil — the equivalent of several hundred dollars. This is a far cry from the huge sums expected in Nea Eleftherohori by a young man who is to inherit land; but what is significant is that before the war such demands were not being made in Kardamili. In those days a landless man would expect no more than a nominal dowry.

Village statistics did not show very convincingly any decrease in the birth rate, however. The decrease in numbers born no more than corresponded to the decline in the village population. Moreover, the decrease in deaths was more rapid than any change in the number of births — owing, mainly, to the elimination of malaria — so that the rate of natural increase of the population had actually risen between 1947 and 1956. So far, it would appear, the villagers have not felt it necessary to change their family customs very profoundly. Migration, facilitated by education, has sufficed to relieve intolerable conditions. The more drastic step of postponing marriage has not become generally necessary.

In poor villages deeper into Mani, these processes have gone much further. In one that I visited only briefly, Yerolimini, I was told that "no" young men are left in the village: all have gone to seek their fortunes in Piraeus, where this village has established a sort of colony of its own. Girls have been left behind, to pine as old maids, or else to marry some boy from one of the even poorer villages high in the hills — boys who are prepared to come down and cultivate the olive trees belonging to the families of the absent young men in return for a share of the crop.

One of the grievances that other Greeks have against the Maniotes (as people from Mani are called), and against the Peloponnesians in general, is that they dominate the civil service of the country. There is some truth in this complaint. The population of these parts has never quarreled with the powers that be; the people are nearly all royalist and conservative. And they cultivate, to a degree remarkable even among the Greeks, a clannishness which leads them to help one another as against natives of other parts of Greece. The gendarmerie, for example, is recruited in disproportionate part from among Maniotes, and the same is true of several other branches of the governmental service. It is, therefore, a bit easier for a person from this section to get a government job than it would be for a man from another part of the country. Villages like Yerolimini make the most of this fact. It looks as though Kardamili, a bit belatedly, is attempting to do the same. But one cannot help wondering what will happen when the graduates of Kardamili and Nea Eleftherohori and of hundreds of similar villages begin to compete for positions in the government. There can hardly be room for them all.

If these six villages were well chosen, if their reactions to the difficulties of the last few years in Greece represent widespread phenomena and not merely local idiosyncracies, then it seems clear that neither American nor Greek official policy has been able to do much to solve the problems of the hill villages. If a peaceable solution is to come, it seems probable that it will come by indirection: that is, by opening opportunities for work in the plains and in the towns even more rapidly than the hill populations increase their numbers. If emigration from the hills reaches a sufficient magnitude, there is a chance that standards of life and expectation derived from urban milieux will penetrate into the hills themselves, and lead the peasants there to change their customs and to regulate their reproduction to an economic standard. But until a lively possibility of attaining or defending such a standard of living begins to open, one cannot expect the hillsmen to abandon old customs which have been deeply bred into them from earliest childhood. In other words, only when self-discipline, parsimony, effort and foresight seem to promise a definitely better life than anything these people now know can changes be expected in the old-fashioned family customs. The difficulty is that the old-fashioned, rough-and-ready — one is tempted to say the natural or automatic — demographic balance has been upset by the comparative efficiency of modern government, and by medical science. Until compensatory adjustments in birth rates have occurred, the result is to create a serious and potentially explosive problem.

It is possible to imagine a time, some twenty or thirty years from now, when a more or less regular pattern of internal migration may establish itself in Greece. Perhaps some day young men from the hills, descending to the plain, may begin as day laborers and in time acquire land, by marriage or by purchase, while the plains villagers restrict their reproduction and send increasing numbers of their sons into town to pursue service or industrial occupations. Or perhaps the more mobile hillsmen may shortcut such a process, and send their sons directly into town occupations, largely bypassing the plains villages as an outlet for their numbers. But as yet only the rudiments of any such migratory pattern can be detected. There still remain, at every level, far too many men who are looking for work or for more work; and only the unusually lucky or energetic can clear the barriers between the paternal village and a wider, freer, more satisfying career elsewhere.

The future of Greece might well be thought of as a race between the natural increase of the hill villages and the capacity of plain and town to absorb men into new productive occupations. The future development of the towns and cities will obviously play a major role in deciding how the race comes out. Accordingly, the next chapter will be devoted to some remarks about conditions in the towns.

THE TOWNS

In spite of the hard times that afflicted Greece from 1930 to 1950, and the persistent economic dislocation that inevitably affected the market economy of towns and cities more seriously than subsistence farming in remote villages, the urban population has grown much faster during the past quarter century than the population of the country as a whole. According to the census classification, which counts as urban every community with 10,000 or more inhabitants, the urban population increased by 883,429, or 46.5 per cent, between 1928 and 1951, while the population of villages and small towns grew by only 423,208, or 9.8 per cent. Moreover, the rate of urban growth has been accelerating relative to the rate of the rest of the population. Whereas between 1928 and 1940 the urban population increased by 449,904 (23.7 per cent), and the rural and small-town population by 690,272 (16.0 per cent), between 1940 and 1951 the former rose by 433,525 (18.4 per cent) but the latter actually dropped by 267,064 (a decline of 5.3 per cent). [1]

These figures should be discounted in some measure, for two reasons. First, census figures in Greece have never been very accurate; underenumeration certainly occurred in the census of 1951, especially in the remoter regions of the country. Hence the rural population was somewhat larger than recorded. Rural underenumeration may, however, have been no greater in 1951 than in earlier censuses. Second, when a town of 9,999 population increased to 10,000 it automatically became a "city," although the addition of one infant did not necessarily alter the occupations of its inhabitants in any significant fashion. Ten towns crossed the statistical borderline between 1928 and 1951, six of them after 1940, and in each case their populations were thereupon subtracted from the small-town category and added to the urban. The changes have consequently not been quite so pronounced as the official statistics suggest.

Yet even when full allowance is made for these factors, it remains true that the growth of urban population in Greece has been comparatively rapid. During the eleven years between 1940 and 1951, the increase of the urban population more than equaled the total population increase. Aside from the widespread desire of young peasant boys to migrate into town, and their not infrequent success in doing so, the major reason for this phenomenon was that wartime loss of life was concentrated

1. Figures derived from National Statistical Services of Greece, *Statistical Yearbook of Greece, 1955*, Athens, 1956, Tables 11 and 12. The populations of the Dodecanese have been subtracted from the published totals in order to keep a constant geographical base, since these islands were annexed to Greece only in 1947.

in the countryside, where guerrilla operations centered, and where famine relief (which operated during the German occupation as well as afterward) was less effective.

On the strength of these statistics one might be inclined to conclude that Greece is already well on the way to solving the problem of rural overpopulation by opening up new jobs in the towns. And indeed, this is so in a sense, even though life in the towns is often very hard and unsatisfactory, especially for those who are still struggling to find a foothold there, after migrating from their native villages. Yet the statistics quoted fail to touch upon a very real problem: the economically parasitical character of the growing towns and cities of Greece. If a preponderant proportion of the new urban population were able to add to the economic production of the country, the trend toward urban growth would augur well for the future. This has not been the case. Too many of the town dwellers make a living by a variety of occupations which do not contribute directly (in some cases not even indirectly) to the general productivity of the society. The urban migration under these circumstances is not quite such a healthy sign. Unless a larger proportion of the towns-people can find economically productive work, there will come a point beyond which the nation will be unable to support its growing number of urban economic parasites.

In some outward aspects, Greek cities resemble cities of western Europe and the United States. Athens and Salonika, at least, can boast a few magnificent boulevards and some handsome new quarters that compare not unfavorably with anything to be found elsewhere. Clothes, too, are of international European style; and if one sees many shabbily dressed people on the streets, one can also find a few very elegantly dressed women, riding in luxurious American cars of the latest model. Equally, the intellectual and cultural life of Athens, and in some degree of lesser centers such as Salonika, may properly be described as an integral part of the larger whole of western European culture. Only the church preserves a peculiarly and uniquely Greek character; yet even the Orthodox Church of Greece, while maintaining its own tradition, has come into a limited contact with Protestant churches of the west through the World Council of Churches.

Yet for all these resemblances, the towns and cities of Greece are still basically different from their counterparts in western countries. The most fundamental difference is that no Greek city can properly be described as an industrial community. Although 2,807,905 persons were classified as urban in the 1951 census, and an additional 1,187,349 as semi-urban, the total factory labor force amounted to less than 100,000; and even if handicraft workers be included, as they were in the official statistics, the total number of persons engaged in manufacturing reached only 296,722. Moreover, this labor force was distributed among no fewer than 81,433 enterprises, making an average of 3.6 employed persons per enterprise. [2] Patently, handicrafts far outweighed industry, and the overwhelming number of "industrial" enterprises were no more than family concerns. A survey by the Greek Federation of Industries in 1950 discovered only fifteen enterprises that employed more than 1,000 persons, and only 235 that employed 100 to 500.

The fact of the matter is that the towns of Greece are little more than market and administrative centers, with a little handicraft added; and the cities are little more than overgrown market and administrative centers, with a little industry and handicraft thrown in. Service occupations of every conceivable sort have undergone an amazing proliferation in the towns, but comparatively few persons are engaged directly in economic production.

Competition for a livelihood is fierce, and nearly every occupation is overcrowded. Where one store could easily handle the

2. Figures derived from *ibid.*, Tables 11, 126, 127, 128.

custom, four or five have sprung up, each doing a small business, and leaving the owner with plenty of spare time during the day to await the next customer. Even high markups do not bring more than a meager living under such circumstances. Doctors and lawyers, especially lawyers, are also often hard put to it to find enough clients to keep them occupied remuneratively. Even though the villages of Greece have an acute shortage of doctors, few persons who have acquired the necessary training are willing to live in a village, even when tempted by a recent government plan whereby any doctor in a rural area is guaranteed a minimum income considerably greater than a beginner can hope to have in town.

Perhaps the greatest superfluity of all is among clerical personnel and white-collar workers, for anyone with secondary school training qualifies for such occupations, whereas the regular professions require further education and storekeeping requires at least a small capital to start with. Nearly all clerical staffs are larger than they need to be, partly because government regulations and laws require private organizations to submit a formidable number of reports and papers for official information, and partly, also, because employers and employees alike prefer sharing the work among a number of persons to working hard with a smaller staff.

A small business, kept within the hands of a single family or group of close relatives, escapes most of this wasteful clerical overhead. In such cases the owner fills out the needful forms in his spare time. Often he neglects to answer official government inquiries, especially if he thinks he may have to pay additional taxes by doing so. His relationship to the official bureaucracy is rather like that of a little fish darting about among the tentacles of an enormous polyp: if he is caught he will be stung, but being far more nimble than the jellyfish, he often escapes.

Larger enterprises, however, cannot escape from constant contact with the tentacles of officialdom. A complicated sym-

biosis is established whereby the enterprise pays taxes and
feeds the official bureaucracy with its indispensable diet of
inked paper while the bureaucracy in turn provides special
favors — tariff protection, government contracts, loans and the
like. Here too there is opportunity for a skillful individual op-
erator to do very well for himself, not so much by escaping
official taxation and regulation as by manipulating them to his
advantage as against rivals. Indeed, the relationship between
the dozen or so really substantial industrial corporations of
Greece and the government is so close that it is not possible, for
instance, for the Bank of Greece to withhold credits or demand
repayment of defaulted loans if such steps threaten bankruptcy.
The government cannot afford to blight industrial enterprises
or throw men out of work; and with official protection, the big
firms do not usually need to worry too much about their productive efficiency or the prices they ask for their products. This
observation is only partially true of the textile industry, where
a rather large number of firms exist, employing nearly half of
the factory labor force of the country, and competing more or
less genuinely among themselves and with foreign factories. Yet
even here, when foreign competition led in 1955 to serious difficulties in the mills, and several thousand workers were dismissed, the government, as already noted, stepped in to raise
the tariff and keep economically marginal factories in operation.

In spite of economy drives which removed about 7,000 officials from the government payroll between 1952 and 1955,
clerical overstaffing was still a feature of the civil service, which
employed 63,000 persons in 1955. It is true that most government offices are very busy, with long lines of petitioners or in-
quirers standing before every door. Yet much of this business
is created by the unwieldiness and complication of official channels, the rigorous centralization of authority, and the almost
irrepressible inclination of every citizen to appeal any unfavor-

able ruling to higher authority. And because the intricacies of the official bureaucracy are so great, a host of private "expediters" has come into existence to help ordinary persons trace their path through the government's red tape and accomplish their business.

In an Athens post office, for example, a person wishing to mail a package is greeted eagerly at the door by some half-dozen young men, each vociferously offering his services as an expediter. When the customer has chosen one of them, the expediter proceeds to fill out the forms required, and presents them to the proper windows in the proper sequence, in return for a small fee. Without such help, it is actually difficult to get a package mailed, for the expediters have the only pens and desk space available, and the officials behind the windows feel that anyone so mean as to try to save the few drachmae involved in a tip to the expediter deserves no sympathy or cooperation from them. In a country where illiteracy is still far from completely abolished, such services of course have greater reason to exist than in other countries; and let it be said to their credit that the young men do get packages mailed more expeditiously than a fully literate person is able to do by himself.

For weightier transactions — tax assessment, customs clearance, sale of real estate or of such an item as an automobile — other specialists are available to help the ordinary citizen find his way through the labyrinth of officialdom. This, indeed, is the great preserve of the legal profession, whose numbers in Greece are far greater, proportionately, than in more highly developed countries of the west.

Quite apart from the army of expediters, the number of persons directly dependent upon government salaries and pensions in the cities of Greece, if calculated, would reach an extraordinary figure. Pensioners of all categories — retired civil servants and army officers, disabled veterans or their widows and orphans, together with old-age pensioners, social security hard-ship cases, and the like — number 250,000 or more. I have been unable to find any figures telling exactly how many persons receive such help from the government, but the budget of 1955 showed expenditures for pensions only slightly smaller than for the salaries of the civil service, and since most pensions are very small, it seems safe to multiply the number of civil servants by four to arrive at an approximation. In addition, the armed forces in 1955 comprised 156,000 men; the civil service, 63,000. If an average of only one dependent for each person receiving a salary or pension from the government is then assumed — and this is certainly a great underestimate — the total arrived at is over 900,000 persons directly dependent upon the government for all or a part of their support.

This figure amounts to a little less than 12 per cent of the entire population of the country, and equals almost one third of all those classified as urban in the census of 1951. Of course, not all of these persons directly dependent upon the government live in towns, and some pensioners and civil servants supplement their income by private enterprises of one sort or another. Nevertheless, it seems safe to assert that more townspeople make a living by qualifying for government salaries or pensions than by working in any of the major branches of the private economy — industry, commerce or transportation.

In the light of figures such as these, it is clear that the villagers of Nea Eleftherohori or Kardamili, when they aim at government jobs for their educated sons, know what they are doing. The outsider, coming to town for the first time, finds it far easier to penetrate the ranks of the government services, where impersonal standards perforce prevail in some measure, than to find a place in some private organization, whose staff is normally and naturally recruited from among relatives of those already holding posts in the firm. And even in the civil service, it helps a great deal to have a relative or friend on the inside who can perhaps step in at the critical moment to influence the choice between equally well qualified candidates.

The Capital City, Athens

The top-heavy character of an urban economy in which governmental salaries and pensions play such a big role and industrial production so slight a part is paralleled by the disproportionate development of the country's capital city, Athens. In 1951, the date of the most recent census, the population of the metropolitan area of Athens was 1,378,586. This amounted to 18 per cent of the population of the entire country. By 1955, the Athens population had probably grown close to one and a half million. This concentration of population in greater Athens is the more remarkable in a country as small and poor as Greece because there are no natural geographical advantages in Attica to account for it. Historical sentiment, which made Athens the capital of the new Greek state in 1833, has resulted in the transformation of what was no more than a biggish village in Turkish times into the present-day metropolis, whereas cities whose geographical situation is far more favorable — cities such as Salonika, Patras or even Volos, each of which commands a comparatively rich natural hinterland — have lagged far behind.

The growth of Athens-Piraeus to its present dimensions must constitute one of the most remarkable victories of political over geographical forces that the world has ever seen, for Athens is located on a small, infertile peninsula, removed from the main lines of natural communication overland and no better situated for sea transport than dozens of other places in Greece.

Athens, of course, has profited from the concentration of government jobs in the central ministries, but this factor by itself has played only a small part in the city's growth. Long before the government payrolls swelled to large proportions, men of wealth and ambition began to come from the provinces, attracted to the game of politics and by the glitter of Athenian life. Then in 1922 and 1923 the size of the city was almost doubled by the sudden influx of refugees from Asia Minor, who settled in a ring of suburbs around the old city. Slightly before this time, and markedly during the interwar years, industry began to cluster in the capital area, partly because the Athens market had become the biggest market in Greece, partly because a special immunity to customs payments on imported fuel made electric power much cheaper in Athens than in the few other towns where it existed, and partly because easy access to the ear of a minister or deputy was at least as important as access to raw materials or labor for any industrialist who wanted his enterprise to flourish. As a modern communications system was built, it inevitably centered in Athens, and this development helped to overcome the natural disadvantages of the location, contributing further to the growth of the capital city.

These factors have continued to operate in recent years, and in spite of some efforts to develop the provinces, and some official concern at the excessive concentration of population, power and wealth in the capital, [3] Athens today dominates the whole country more completely than it did a decade ago. Improved communications have played a major part in this phenomenon, together with the general expansion of governmental functions.

One of the striking paradoxes of present-day Athens is its modernity. The brick and mortar of Athens is, on the average, far newer than that of New York or Chicago. Not only suburbs, which stretch for miles in all directions, but the center of the city, too, has been built or rebuilt within the past thirty-five

3. A survey by the Greek Federation of Industries in 1950 found that 59 per cent of the nation's factory labor force was concentrated in the capital area.

years; and a surprising number of structures have been put up since 1950. Official statistics show that Athens, with about 18 per cent of the nation's population, nevertheless was the seat of roughly half of all building activity between 1950 and 1955. More than half of all building permits for houses and apartments were issued for the capital area during these years; and Athens' share of new stores, factories and government buildings was only slightly under 50 per cent. [4] With so much new construction in progress, any casual visitor is bound to conclude that the city is booming; and in its own fashion it is.

Yet for many Athenians life is desperately difficult. For as long as anyone cares to remember, prices have been edging up month by month, the increase averaging nearly 10 per cent a year between 1950 and 1955. [5] Incomes, even when secure, cannot easily be made to keep up. For a large part of the population, incomes are anything but secure. The extensive building activity offers a very considerable source of employment, but such employment is seasonal, and a contractor can always find half a dozen applicants among whom to choose, in case a man falls ill or objects to the wages or conditions of work offered.

It is true that government regulations prescribe a minimum wage of 30 drachmae a day — equivalent to $1 at official rates of exchange, and worth somewhat more in local purchasing power. But this is a rate upon which a single man can exist only meagerly and a family man can scarcely live at all. It is also true that unemployment insurance, medical insurance and a variety of other social security benefits are available to the urban workingman, and these certainly help to cushion the hardships of his life. But they do not suffice to make his life easy.

Cases of serious malnutrition, due to dire poverty, are easily discovered in the poor suburbs of the city. One family I visited,

4. *Statistical Yearbook of Greece, 1955*, Tables 139, 141.
5. *Ibid.*, Table 213.

for example, consisted of a mother, two daughters and an infant grandchild. The father was tubercular, and lived in a government sanitarium; the young girl's husband (she was about eighteen) was away in the army doing his military service. He apparently sent them little or nothing from his army pay, and the family existed on a pittance paid the mother by the social security agency of the government. The baby, particularly, was a pitiful sight, thin and weak, and extraordinarily retarded for its age by chronic undernourishment. The whole family was hungry; and in winter the two cubbyholes in which they lived must become bitter chill and miserable. Three out of five children had already died, one by violence in 1945, the others from tuberculosis. The conditions under which the survivors existed made it all too probable that tuberculosis or some other disease would strike them down, too.

The prewar history of this family was not untypical of Athenian working-class families. Both father and mother were refugees from Asia Minor. The father had become a baker, and when he had work the family fared not too badly. But even before the war, tuberculosis plagued the family, and the father had a bout of disability in the late 1930's. After that he attempted to branch out into business on his own, opening a *taverna* (a restaurant and wineshop) by converting the larger part of his house to public use. But the venture did not flourish, and the *taverna* was closed. The room was vacant since there was no furniture for it, and the mother hoped rather vaguely to be able to rent it to someone who might open the *taverna* again.

The father's eagerness to get into business for himself and his distaste for working for a stranger's wages are thoroughly characteristic of Greeks of every social class. These attitudes help to explain the remarkable success Greeks have always had when living as aliens in a society where individual enterprise is less firmly rooted in popular psychology. On the other hand, in a homogeneous Greek society, composed almost entirely of would-be entrepreneurs, wasteful duplication of services and unprofitable ventures like the family *taverna* become very conspicuous.

The dire straits into which this family had fallen are not so very unusual. Illness or unemployment or a disastrous business venture threatens almost every Athenian family with something similar. But in one important respect the condition of this family was worse than normal: they lacked relatives who might have helped them. Governmental assistance is barely enough to keep body and soul together, but an average family, facing such a crisis, would have brothers or cousins or other relatives who could be counted on to help relieve the hardship. The extraordinarily tight-knit character of Greek family life, in comparison with family attitudes current in the United States or in western Europe, here finds a justification and, perhaps, its historical explanation. It was by privately helping one another in time of hardship that Greeks became the major urban business and professional class of the Ottoman Empire. Under the comparatively primitive economic and occasionally erratic political conditions of that empire, high profits alternated with unforeseeable disasters. The practical effect of the sense of obligation between even rather remote relatives was to create a sort of informal "mutual insurance" system to cushion the effects of periodic disasters. Even though new-fangled notions of government social insurance and other services have been accepted during the last two decades, the age-old "family insurance" system of Greece continues to work with almost undiminished vigor.

And with an irony not perhaps unusual in social relationships, this survival, while it immeasurably helps in particular cases, is closely intertwined with the basic cause of most of the country's economic difficulties: overpopulation. For the old-fashioned desire for early marriages and large families helps to assure the smooth working of the "mutual insurance" system, spreading risks widely and diminishing the burden of any single disaster on any particular person or family.

Moreover, the tight-knit family ties militate powerfully against efficiency in larger social groupings of a sort required for the free functioning of modern technology, especially in the industrial field. All too often old virtues have become, not perhaps vices, but socially disadvantageous practices. Presumably these disproportions arise from the fact that the rapid assimilation of western technology and culture in the past century and a half has not allowed time for old social attitudes to adjust to the new conditions and transform themselves slowly, piecemeal, and without conscious direction or control.

The circumstances under which the baker's family existed were so debilitating to mind and body as to deprive the members of the family of any but sporadic capacity to protest. In terms of their effect upon the social and political stability of the country, such extreme cases, however great the suffering, are not important. The victims lack the energy to do very much.

This lassitude is not true of others, especially of young men who have acquired a secondary school education and then been unable to find a job that accords with their expectations. The case of one young man, whom I met only briefly, may be taken as representative of this group. He had a wife and child, and expected a second child in a few months. He had been through gymnasium, and had served as a reserve officer in the army. Upon demobilization, however, he had been unable to find any work better than that offered him by a construction contractor — filling the maw of a concrete mixer to supply concrete for one of the handsome new apartment buildings of the city. He was young and strong, and the physical labor was not in itself what he resented. But to work under a man whom he felt to be his natural inferior — for the contractor had not been to gymnasium

— and to know that any outward expression of that resentment would mean the abrupt end of his employment, this he found almost intolerable. In addition, there was the all too real difficulty of making ends meet on the wages he received. What would happen when the second child arrived he did not know and did not like to think about.

Actually, he had not yet given up hope of finding a job more suited to his education and expectations. He had friends and relatives whose influence had already been mobilized to find him something better, but all efforts had so far been in vain. He knew English, and his hopes were centered on getting a post as interpreter with an American corporation that was negotiating for a permit to build a luxury hotel in Athens. The basis of his hope was that he had a friend who was acquainted with one of the Americans behind this project. Communism was anathema to him, yet discontent was boiling within him, and his feelings toward his employer were little short of hatred.

Once again, this young man represents an extreme case. Most of those who have been through secondary school manage to avoid heavy physical labor such as he was doing. Yet the majority of those who succeed in finding some sort of white-collar work still feel discontent. They find it hard to live on their meager salaries; they regard their bosses as incompetent or overbearing; and they do not often subordinate themselves gladly.

I recall an evening's conversation with a group of comparatively well-to-do salaried employees, several of whom owned the small homes in which they lived, and all of whom had held steady jobs through the troubled postwar period. Yet in spite of their hard-won status and comparative security, all found reason to criticize the government and their immediate bosses. They seemed to have a deep-seated feeling that someone was cheating them of their just deserts; that the government repre-

sented interests other than their own; that ill will and selfish-
ness on the part of the "rich" accounted for most of the economic troubles of their country; that social justice was not to
be found in Greece. The more articulate among them had
grasped firmly the idea that poverty could be eradicated by
government action, in Greece as much as elsewhere, but they
had quite failed to understand the obstacles in the way of any
such dream. Instead, they fell back upon rather vague, but
heartfelt, moral condemnation of the people who were running
things.

A similar spirit is, I believe, very widespread among the educated and semi-educated groups in Athens and in the country
at large. The propaganda of the national government, which
for long years publicized grandiose plans for economic reconstruction, and the promises so confidently held out in times
past by Communists and fellow travelers have combined to convince these people that the social order is capable of relatively
easy reconstruction through conscious and deliberate action.
And since they have been persuaded that the forms of society
and economy are not natural but man-made, and have observed
that what they see about them is far from satisfactory, they have
concluded, logically enough, that ill will is somewhere at work
to distort reality, and deprive their hopes and dreams of just
fruition.

The men with whom I talked were vague and inexact when
questioned as to what persons were at fault; they were even
more vague when asked who might set matters right, or how it
could be done. Yet these uncertainties did not detract from the
depth of their feeling against the existing state of affairs.

Attitudes such as these naturally find ready response in the
minds of the working class, for the frustrations and hardships
confronting the white-collar and professional groups in Athenian society are only mitigated versions of the frustrations and

hardships endured by manual laborers. The result is that in the larger cities of Greece, in Athens and Salonika in particular, where these two classes constitute a majority of the population, leftist or at any rate anti-government parties have regularly won the largest slice of the vote in postwar elections.

In general, the Athenians know what they are against, but seem to have no very clear idea of what they are for. Even those who support conservative and royalist parties at the polls tend to do so as a protest against the political alternative they are offered, rather than out of a positive acceptance of programs or leaders. When Papagos was alive and led his Rally this was less true, since the magic of his name attracted a degree of positive support. This, however, was a purely personal phenomenon, and his successor, Constantine Karamanlis, has not been able to transfer any significant share of the General's charisma to himself.

Hence if one looks for supporters of the status quo in Athens (or outside the city, for that matter) one finds them hard to discover. Even men of property — of whom there are a significant, even if statistically small, number in Athens — are more likely to complain of the high level of taxation and of the ineffectiveness of the government on the Cyprus question than they are to sing the prime minister's praises. Yet men of property naturally do have an interest in maintaining the existing social order of the country, and are inclined to feel that although it is not, perhaps, good, nevertheless it is certainly better than any visible alternative.

Three more or less distinct groups stand out among the elite class of Athens. First, there are a few families whose wealth and social and political prominence go back for several generations, characteristically to the days of the Greek War of Independence. Until 1910, these families enjoyed a near-monopoly of political leadership, owing to traditional ties between the peasants of particular regions of the country and one or another such family. The relationship was almost patriarchal — in some districts it was definitely tribal. That is to say, one of the "great" families would mediate between the villagers of his district and the officials of the government whenever something came up that called for intervention; he might help "his" peasants out in time of special crisis with loans or hospitality, and in return he could count upon their votes for candidates of his choice at election time. This system broke down in 1910 when new urban groups came to political power behind Eleftherios Venizelos; it was further eroded between the wars and almost entirely disintegrated during World War II. Only a few traces remain today. The old families have lost control even of the royalist parties. Some of their members remain active in politics, but when successful, do so on a new basis, relying not on traditional ties to a locality, but on the general stock-in-trade of Greek politics — Cyprus, Communism, favors to supporters and the like.

These old families were once extensive landowners, but even during the nineteenth century much of their land was sold to peasants, and with the land reforms of the twentieth century the former basis of their economic and social position was entirely, or almost entirely, surrendered. Instead, their wealth was invested in stocks and bonds — often mainly foreign stocks and bonds — and in urban real estate or shipping. The group is not much like the aristocracies of western Europe, since it lacks ancient ancestry and has no disdain for commerce or business. Quite the contrary, its members regularly dabble in business — even if minor ventures, such as importing foreign commodities, constitute only a small part of their income.

Nevertheless, the old families have played a role somewhat analogous to that of European aristocracies in their relationship to the King and his court. They were among the mainstays of royalism in Greece during the years between 1915 and 1949, when the monarch's status was a burning political question. The personal associates of the royal family continue to be largely drawn from this group. [6] And since the King exercises a considerable constitutional power in Greece, and can occasionally exert a decisive voice in the by-play of politics (as, for example, when he chose Karamanlis to succeed to the premiership in 1955), the political influence of the old families has remained greater than their numbers or outward appearance might suggest.

A second layer of the elite is that associated with the Venizelist movement of 1910–35. Many persons who lacked traditional status but had acquired wealth in commerce or otherwise were attracted to the Venizelist standard — a standard which became republican after 1923. A small number of the older elite, especially shipowners, also joined Venizelos' party. These families remain, even today, perceptibly distinct from their "royalist" counterparts. The gap is narrowing, however, and has lost the bitterness with which it was fraught as recently as 1944 or 1945.

A third group are the *nouveaux riches:* persons who, by hook or by crook, rose to positions of affluence during the war and postwar years. There are not many of them, and their methods have been distinctly questionable, for in a time of general economic disorganization, wealth can only be acquired by trading

6. Because the Ionian Islands had been a part of the medieval and early modern Venetian empire, a European type of aristocracy grew up on those islands, especially on the richest and most important of them, Corfu. Corfiote families, with this genuine aristocratic background, have played a rather prominent part in the court circle of Greece in the postwar period, perhaps because the royal family has felt most completely at home in such company.

upon widespread suffering. Yet *nouveaux riches* do exist, and they are trying hard to win social acceptance among the older families by being more royalist than the King, and more genteel than the old families.

A question very difficult to answer satisfactorily is what real influence the rich have upon the policies of the government. Prominent politicians, by virtue of their prominence, have won access to the charmed circle of Athenian high society. This may often involve a degree of seduction from radicalism. Certainly more than one ambitious young man has found it possible to marry above himself on the strength of his political prowess. Moreover, party finances and election expenses depend largely upon private donations. This means that wealthy persons have a chance to play a disproportionate role in influencing political parties. The importance of the King and his circle of advisers has already been mentioned.

More significant than these means of affecting the personalities and policies of government is the relationship between money and newspapers. Newspaper publicity and commendation constitute an almost indispensable item in any successful political career. This, more than any other, is the way a man's name comes to the public eye; and some of the Athens newspapers which enjoy a national circulation are thoroughly venal. Yet there are several Athens newspapers that aim at popularity and circulation by following a leftist line, and one in 1956 seemed to be a Communist sheet in all but name. Moreover, some of the most rabidly nationalist and conservative papers criticized the government so unmercifully for its supine attitude on Cyprus that, by the violence with which they belabored established authorities, they in effect appealed to discontented, radical opinion.

The distribution of newspapers across the political spectrum corresponds to the general fact that Greece is a democratic country in the political sense. Politicians, in or out of office, have to appeal to the general mass of the electorate as best they can; and since the electorate generally dislikes and distrusts men of wealth, politicians cannot really accept the control of such a small minority and survive, even though a rising young politician may visit the salons and solicit the money of Athenian high society, and enjoy the flattery of social success in the capital.

In general, the relationship between government and the wealthy class of Athens is, I suspect, less significant on the political than on the administrative level. It is on this level that civil servants and business entrepreneurs come into real contact, as the officials undertake to apply some law or regulation to particular cases and transactions. Here taxes are paid or not paid; here permits are given or refused; here loans and tariffs and fees are decided upon. And here, also, bribes are offered and taken. In all such contacts, men of wealth have real advantages over those who lack money, and the most unscrupulous often have the greatest advantages.

Yet although these strictures are certainly true, it is also true that the ministers and civil servants of the Greek government are not always willing to cooperate with men of private wealth. Particularly during the first year or so of Papagos' regime, a genuinely radical spirit permeated the most important levels of the key economic ministries, a spirit which was highly critical of the failure of private capital to plunge into industrial development, and led in many instances to the levying of hitherto unheard-of taxes against wealthy persons. This aggressive attitude subsided somewhat in 1955 and 1956 but it did not entirely die away.

The exigencies of winning votes from a population which is far from wealthy and is highly critical of the few who do own property, require politicians, no matter what their position in

the political spectrum may be, to promise tax and other reforms aimed against the rich; and almost equally important, the
practical problems which arise when officials attempt to do
something constructive about the lopsided economy of the
country also impel them to impinge upon the traditional privileges and advantages men of wealth formerly enjoyed in
Greece. Taxes and regulations governing the uses to be made
of private capital are legion, and even if they are not always
equally enforced, the efforts which are made to enforce such
laws do restrict and diminish what not so many years ago were
regarded as sacred and unquestioned rights of property.

Like other capitalist countries during the past two decades,
Greece has moved rapidly toward what would once have been
described as socialism. The effect of the American aid programs, which have been administered through the Greek government and often by it, has been an acceleration of the growth
and a broadening of the scope of governmental regulation and
control. To be sure, private ownership of industrial capital continues, but the real scope of what a private owner can or wishes
to do with his property is markedly reduced. The economy is
well on its way to becoming a political economy, in which
strictly economic or financial calculations and advantages are
checked and often countermanded by distinctly political considerations: considerations both of votes and of what officials
think may be the general good of the nation. Nor is this *rap-
prochement* between officialdom and politicians on the one
hand and property owners on the other entirely a case of ag-
gression by the government. The advantages a private firm can
gain from close association with officialdom are very real, and
many businessmen gladly pay the price of submitting to closer
and closer regulation in order to receive such advantages — indeed, struggle to gain them.

Nevertheless, it must be borne in mind that a great gap often exists between what is written on the law books or in government regulations and what actually happens. Ways through and around the law have always been more important in Greece than in some other countries, and this perviousness of the law means, especially for small entrepreneurs, that political control of business operations is very much reduced.

The Provincial Towns

The rise of Athens to megalopolitan dimensions, and the improvement of overland transport which has made such growth possible, have had a blighting effect upon many provincial towns, especially upon small ports that formerly served as outlets for regional surpluses and received goods brought by sea for distribution inland. Until quite recently, the small coastal vessels which plied the Aegean and Ionian seas constituted an absolutely vital means of transportation for large parts of Greece. After 1950, the extension of the road system deprived these vessels of much of their former trade, since trucks could nearly always do the job better, and could deliver the goods directly to their destination without further loading or unloading. For the same reason, even tramp steamers have tended in recent years to prefer making a single call at Piraeus to putting in two or three times at lesser ports to unload or take on small bits of cargo. Hence, the ports of cities like Volos, Kavalla or Kalamata have not prospered; only Salonika and, to a lesser degree, Patras have been able to retain some of their old importance.

Salonika is designed by nature to be one of the three greatest cities of the Balkan peninsula. Only Constantinople and Belgrade can rival the natural advantages of its location, for it lies at the juncture of two of the major routes of transport through the Balkans: the ancient Via Egnatia of the Romans, from

Durazzo to Constantinople, and the Vardar-Morava route northward to Belgrade, which the railroad follows. But international boundaries erected in 1913 after the second Balkan war cut Salonika off from most of its natural hinterland; and the economic nationalism of the interwar years, together with the ideological tensions between Greece and its northern neighbors in the post-World War II period, drastically reduced movement of goods across these frontiers.

Yet Salonika has a history and tradition as a great city going back to Roman and Byzantine times. This tradition has not entirely been eclipsed by Athens' octopus-like grasp. The fact that Salonika is rather more than three hundred miles distant from Athens by road also has helped to keep the city independent. A real "Macedonian" consciousness has existed in northern Greece, a sense of being different from the south (as it is), mingled sometimes with a grievance (less clearly justified) at the exploitation of Macedonian wealth by the south. Salonika has served as the natural focus for all these feelings. The fact that it alone maintains a newspaper press that can compete with the Athens papers is perhaps the best index of the reality of Salonika's status as an independent urban center. Salonika is also the seat of the country's only provincial university; and in conformity to a very old tradition, an international fair is held every year in Salonika, which even Athenians sometimes find worth visiting. Since 1951, the city has seen a building boom smaller than, but comparable to, that of Athens.

From Turkish times, Salonika and two nearby towns in central Macedonia, Naousa and Edessa, have been the seats of a fairly important textile industry. This industry survived the war, though many of the factories were among the most antiquated and inefficient of the country. In recent years, some new industry has also been established in Salonika — an agricultural machinery plant, for example. But perhaps the most significant new economic development is the beginning of rail shipment of fresh fruit to Germany. Only relatively small quantities of grapes, peaches and apples were shipped in 1955 and 1956, but prices received in Germany made the trade highly attractive, and plans for enlarging the volume of export are under way. Two things make this departure possible: the cooperation of the Yugoslav railroads, and the introduction of a chemical spray which preserves the fruit even in unrefrigerated cars for the length of time required to reach German markets.

If this trade can be expanded in future years, it seems to offer one of the most promising means of raising the economic level of the country generally, and of bringing to Salonika in particular some part of the role its geographical situation implies. The climate of Greece opens the possibility of making the country a southern California for northern Europe; and the intensive labor required for large-scale market gardening and fruit farming offers potential employment for some of the surplus population from which Greece now suffers, employment both on farms and along the way, in packing, processing, grading and shipping.

The development of a market for Greek fruit in Germany has also been facilitated by diplomatic and technical assistance offered by the Greek government to the private merchants who conduct the trade. Yet government policy, by and large, has been to emphasize industry, and down to 1956 officials were allowing or even encouraging the growing concentration of industry in the capital area. With the completion of the electric grid system in 1955, however, and with the relaxation of the American aid mission's prohibition against committing funds for new projects, the government began to go ahead with plans for the creation of a new provincial industrial center in western

Macedonia, near the town of Ptolemais. In 1956, nearly everything still remained in the blueprint stage, and there was no
certainty that all the financial and technical obstacles would be
safely surmounted. But plans at least called for the opening of
large-scale lignite mines, the construction of a plant to turn the
raw lignite into briquettes, and the use of this fuel to feed a
large generating plant. In addition, a fertilizer plant was to be
constructed to produce nitrogenous fertilizers which have hitherto been imported; and it was hoped that private industries
could be attracted to the site, by the availability of cheap fuel,
abundant electric power and various chemical by-products of
the lignite. Plans called for the completion of the mine, bri-
quette plant, power station and fertilizer factory by 1960, but
it will be surprising if the schedule is actually realized. Nevertheless, if the government's plans do come to fruition, Ptolemais
will emerge in a few years as a new and technically very modern industrial center, something Greece has never seen before
even in the capital area.

A less ambitious project, but one which was actually nearing
completion in 1956, was the development of a nickel-processing
plant not far north of Lamia in central Greece. Export of partly
refined nickeliferous metal began in the summer of 1956, and
was scheduled to increase as new furnaces came into operation
during the following months.

Other possibilities for mining and industrial development
exist in other provincial areas, but problems of finding the initial capital and questions of probable costs in relation to world
market levels make these potentialities academic, at least in the
immediate future. Two of the most lively of the projects under
discussion in 1956 were the mining of asbestos in an area near
Kozani in western Macedonia — a possibility that has interested
the Kennecott Copper Corporation — and the production of

aluminum with electric power to be provided by a dam on the Acheloos River in western Greece.

If and when these projects and others like them become fact, Greece will begin to have a variegated and geographically dispersed industrial plant, an asset the country definitely lacks at present. For the time being, with the few exceptions mentioned, the provincial towns of Greece remain commercial, handicraft and administrative centers, but no more. Some of the towns have grown rather rapidly in recent years, and seem to be flourishing so far as very superficial observation can discern. Katerini, for example, the commercial center nearest to Nea Eleftherohori, increased its population between 1940 and 1951 by nearly one half [7] and has certainly continued to grow since the last census was taken. Its prosperity rests largely upon trade with the surrounding villages, but the fact that an important army garrison is stationed there is an additional asset to the town. Fresh paint, new store fronts, a remarkably attractive municipal park and the bustle of the business streets lend the town an air of prosperity that is rare in the provinces.

By comparison, the larger and intrinsically more important town of Larissa, the inland metropolis of the Thessalian plain and a market center for Lofiscos, seems to have undergone little change since 1947. Larissa, too, has grown, though more slowly than Katerini. Its population increased by more than 25 per cent between 1940 and 1951, [8] but this growth has not been reflected in an improved appearance of the central streets. It may be that the merchants of Larissa share with the peasants of Lofiscos a distaste for living up to their means, or perhaps the relatively slow development of more intensive farming in the

7. *Statistical Yearbook of Greece, 1955,* Table 10. The exact increase was 45.3 per cent, from 16,938 to 24,605.
8. *Ibid.*

Thessalian plain conduces to a slower increase in the business of the towns serving that district. At any rate, the outward contrast between Katerini and Larissa suggests that where the plains villages have gone furthest in improving the technical level of their agriculture, the prosperity of the local market towns has likewise increased most markedly. This is no more than one would expect.

Smaller centers, which played a role in days when transport was more primitive, have generally suffered decline, if not in population then certainly in prosperity. This has been the case, for example, with towns such as Gythion and Sparta in the Peloponnese. Gythion, a port near the mouth of the Eurotas River, used to serve as the major outlet for the products of the valley, transshipping olive oil, oranges and similar goods to Athens or other markets. New roads have deprived the town of most of its former function. The stream of traffic no longer runs southward to the coast, but northward directly to Tripolis or Athens, leaving Gythion isolated, remote and idle. Sparta, bearing a name so famous in history, has continued to enjoy an income from tourists, and has the further advantage of being the ancestral birthplace of a large number of emigrants who have prospered overseas, especially in the United States. Yet its function as a market center for the middle section of the Eurotas valley has undergone considerable decline, owing to the facility with which trucks can travel directly from the villages to larger centers like Tripolis or Athens.

In general, therefore, it can be said that during recent years big towns have been outstripping smaller ones, and the one big city of Greece has been leaving its provincial rivals farther and farther behind. Regional market towns have prospered in proportion as the villages around them have prospered; lesser centers, particularly minor ports, have suffered decline; and urban industrialism outside Athens has made little headway, although plans for the development of modern industry in a few provincial centers are being actively pressed by the government.

The major problem at present is not so much urbanization per se. This is proceeding apace. Rather it is to find economically productive work for a larger proportion of the urban population. The Greek government's answer has been industrialization, as fast as might be. This has the disadvantage of being expensive; it has the further disadvantage of requiring, in the absence of a ready and sufficient supply of private capital, that the government itself take the initiative and responsibility for industrial investment. This puts a considerable strain upon the administrative system of the country. How well the government and civil service will be able to support the strain depends upon the character of Greek public life, and upon the nation's international relations. Observations on these matters follow in the next chapter.

CHAPTER 5

PUBLIC LIFE

Public Administration

A leading official of the American economic mission in Greece said to me, when I asked about the efficiency of Greek administration: "We got absolutely nowhere trying to improve the civil service. It's the same as ever; but then, if all those people were not drawing government salaries, they would be on relief, so perhaps it doesn't make very much difference." The young man had been in Greece for a little more than a year, and during that time it was perhaps true that no very perceptible changes had come to the Greek administrative machine. Over a longer period, however, important changes have taken place. In particular, a group of comparatively youthful economists and statisticians have risen to key posts in many of the ministries, and are able to advise their superiors in the light of a type of professional training and in accordance with intellectual concepts which ten years ago were noticeably absent from the policy-making levels of the Greek civil service. Even if the execution of official policy is not always effective, ideas of what government ought to do and can do and how to go about doing it have undergone radical change.

Politicians and civil servants of the immediate postwar period in Greece grew up in a time when society and the economy were expected to run themselves, subject only to sporadic official interference. The painful inadequacy of this outlook became apparent in 1947, when the emergency relief and reconstruction undertaken by UNRRA began to taper off before the economy had been restored to running order. In this situation, the Greek government lacked ideas as much as the means with which to try to cope with the problems confronting the country. All too clearly, automatic restoration to something like the prewar social and economic pattern was out of the question. Planning and massive organization of effort by government agencies were still needed if serious collapse was to be avoided.

The American aid mission, to be sure, stepped into the gap created by the withdrawal of the British and of UNRRA, and attempted far more energetically than its predecessors to educate Greek administrative personnel to new ways of thinking. Even before 1947, foreigners — mostly American and British — had insisted on making plans for the development of the Greek economy, and a small number of Greeks had been drawn into the attempt. Yet by and large, it was the foreigners who made plans, and the Greeks were consulted afterward. This remained more or less the case until 1950 or 1951; but in proportion as the Americans reduced the scale of their economic aid after 1952 and withdrew from detailed supervision of the ministries, the task of making plans was transferred to Greek hands.

Some senior Greek civil servants, veterans from 1945 and 1946, welcomed the new scope and authority thus entrusted to them; but in the main the men who inherited the new role were not the same persons who ten or even five years before had occupied leading positions in the Greek civil service. Between 1947 and 1952, when American advisers were introduced into nearly all Greek ministries, these impatient foreigners were able to play a major part in determining promotions and key personnel assignments within the ministries. Many a young American economist found himself at first dealing with men much older than himself, men whose ideas often had little relation to those he had imbibed during graduate training in some American university. This regularly led to serious friction, for senior Greek officials were not much inclined to go to school to cocksure youths scarcely more than half their own age. But bright young men could be found in the lower ranks of the civil service who either already shared the concepts of their American counterparts or quickly acquired some familiarity with them. Many such men were sent to the United States for additional technical training, or visited Washington to observe American administrative methods at first hand.

These persons naturally seemed to the Americans to be just the type to run things; and the voice of an American adviser was sufficiently powerful to secure rapid advancement for men he favored. In this fashion a new generation of officials came rapidly to the fore within the Greek ministries, while many of their former superiors were shunted off to unimportant posts or else retired.

By 1956, therefore, the economic ministries of the Greek civil service were sprinkled with men of a quite new type, sometimes of high ability and energy, many of them well at home in the language of post-Keynesian economics. A national statistical service was organized to provide them with data for their calculations; and innumerable plans and surveys were made, priorities agreed upon, and projects for future expansion worked out in varying degrees of detail.

Two aims dominated most of the planning of these men. One was to improve the country's balance of payments, partly by producing goods domestically that had hitherto been imported, and partly by developing new exports (especially minerals) or enlarging old ones. The second general aim was to expand employment. Military considerations figured only indirectly in their calculations, and helping political and personal friends or penalizing opponents played almost no role at all. This was a great departure, for in the prewar years, whatever economic planning the Greek government had undertaken was heavily colored by these calculations, and paid little attention to broader aims which were assumed to be beyond deliberate manipulation.

Conversations with representatives of this rising group of civil servants gave me the impression that they were more buoyantly optimistic about the future of Greece than the American economists in the aid mission. Greek economic planners were not much inclined to worry about inflation and disbalanced government budgets: they wanted to see new dams, irrigation canals, factories and mines, and felt that if inflation was the easiest way to finance the internal costs of such construction, then inflation was preferable to standing still and waiting until private savings or a government surplus was on hand to pay for the new investment. I also gained the impression that they felt themselves embarked upon a new adventure: striving for conscious management of the direction and pace of economic growth on a nation-wide basis. Moreover, they found the game of manipulating the levers from behind the scenes a fascinating and entirely absorbing enterprise — advising ministers, talking back to the Americans, and, as they hoped, saving their country from age-old poverty and hopelessness.

Whether their optimism was well founded, and whether or not the priorities the Greeks have decided upon are the best, seem to me a good deal less important than the fact that such a spirit was abroad at all. Mistakes have been made, and will almost surely be made in the future; but the great mistake which paralyzed the government of Greece in the first postwar years — the mistake of not knowing what to do, of having no policy but one of inaction, of waiting for things to pick up by themselves — this mistake at least will not be made as long as the new generation of civil servants remains as a leaven in the economic ministries, and ministers accept their advice. This is a great change from 1945 or 1946, one for which the American economic mission can take a major share of the credit.

The transformation of the upper ranges of the bureaucracy in the central ministries in Athens was only faintly reflected in the lower ranks in 1956. In general, a petty official sitting behind his desk continued to exhibit a displeasing servility toward his superiors (at least to their faces) and a corresponding hauteur in dealing with mere members of the public. The besetting weakness of Greek administration has been the unwillingness of superiors to delegate much responsibility to their subordinates, and this feature seemed as strong as ever. Busywork, created by passing papers over a long series of desks for approval or initialing, up and again down the hierarchy of rank, was a feature of many government offices, so much so that it was hard not to believe that official routings had been designed to keep a lot of people occupied rather than to get decisions made. It was this feature of Greek administration that the

American economist of the aid mission had in mind when he declared that nothing had changed in the civil service.

In dealing with the public, Greek civil servants often gave a most unfavorable impression. Aside from the airs they assumed as representatives of authority and power, they frequently seemed not in the least concerned to help an individual solve a problem or attain something to which he was legally entitled. Instead, petty details of paper work — making application with all the correct verbiage on sheets of paper of the right size for easy filing, and so on — these were what seemed to matter; and I felt, more than once, that when an official found some flaw in the papers submitted to him, he took a certain pleasure in rejecting them and ordering the applicant to return some other time with the red tape properly tinted.

Correctness in details of this sort did, of course, assist in making clerical routine easy, but this was not, I feel sure, the compelling motive. Rather, insistence upon jots and tittles protected a subordinate from criticism by his superior, and at the same time gave him a satisfying sense of his own power as against the public.

On the other hand, when an important man — that is, someone with connections higher up — came along, he claimed and received very special treatment. He was privileged to follow his papers into the inner sanctums of senior officials, thus making sure that prompt action was taken on them. Obstacles were smoothed over and procedural rules were sometimes suspended for a man with influential friends. Foreigners often, though not always, were given the same sort of red-carpet treatment, and were accorded privileges and deference withheld from ordinary Greeks.

When a private person had business with a government agency, he would first try to find someone who knew someone in the office concerned, in order to open a door for prompt and courteous service by means of private communication. As a result, a comparatively small number of persons whose social position or family connections gave them an inside track enjoyed a great advantage in dealings with officialdom, while the poor and friendless could hardly regard the government machine as anything but an obstacle between themselves and their legal rights.

The idea that officials should be public servants rather than public masters has never been firmly rooted in modern Greece. Byzantine and Turkish tradition, transformed according to Bavarian and then German models, shaped the civil service; and the fact that educated persons regard themselves as elevated far above their ignorant fellows has reinforced and perpetuated the old dichotomy between official and subject.

It must be said that the fault has not lain entirely with the civil servants. The ordinary private citizen in Greece is prone to look upon the government as his natural enemy — a group of men who are out to tax him and interfere with what he wants to do. It follows that almost any device to foil the agents of the government is considered legitimate — deceit, lying, bribery or just the exertion of "influence." Indeed, almost all Greeks entertain a kind of admiration for a man who is clever or bold or lucky enough to get around the law and the bureaucracy. Sense of duty to public authorities and laws has never been very strong in the country. More than most nations, the Greeks remain anarchists and individualists at heart; and rather high-handed methods, together with rigid punctiliousness in matters of red tape, is a natural and perhaps almost inevitable official response to such public attitudes.

A few segments of the bureaucracy, however, were making serious efforts to serve the public. The most conspicuous of these were the agricultural extension agents, whose contacts with the farmers seemed to be genuinely friendly and highly effective in nearly all of the villages I visited. Here again, the American aid mission was entitled to a great deal of credit, for American advisers had made special efforts to reorganize the agricultural extension service on the model of the county agricultural agents in the United States. Many of the Greek agriculturalists had been sent to study in America before receiving their appointments. The public health agencies were another branch of the central administration in which a spirit of service had come to prevail; and there may have been others. In general, it was the older departments of the government, and particularly those concerned with money and taxes, in which the unpleasant but traditional attitudes were most firmly and universally established.

Another administrative change, and one which produced highly beneficial results in some localities at least, was the reinvigoration of local government. During the war and afterward, until 1951, local government officials were appointed through the Ministry of Interior. In 1951, however, local elections were organized, partly at least in response to repeated urging from Americans. As a result of these elections, village presidents and city mayors, together with advisory councils which assisted them in their administration, became more nearly independent of the central government, and commanded, presumably, more local confidence and support than was likely to be the case when the offices were filled by appointment from above.

The system did not always work smoothly — witness Cherasia; but my impression of the local officials whom I met in 1956 was on the whole a quite favorable one. Except in Cherasia, the village presidents seemed to have the full confidence of the villagers, and some of them were men of real intelligence and force of character. The president of Old Corinth would be a distinguished man in any company. Authority seemed to rest as naturally upon his shoulders as the callouses rested upon his palms. This easy relation between village officers and the people of their community had definitely not been characteristic in 1947.

Local government in Greece was suffering, however, from a chronic and serious handicap. Local authorities lacked funds, and could seldom do anything beyond routine administration without borrowing from some agency of the central government. [1] The result of this situation was to extend greatly the real authority and influence of the central government over local affairs. Village and municipal authorities spent a great deal of time waiting in the anterooms of officials of the central government in the hope of securing money with which to carry through some local improvement.

Villages had always depended on the Agricultural Bank or on one of the central ministries for finding money for any important project; cities and towns until 1949 had financed their local expenditures mainly through excise duties imposed upon goods brought into the municipality. Before that year, long lines of peasant carts, waiting their turn at municipal excise stations, were a frequent sight in the outskirts of every town. Internal tariffs were abolished in 1949, however, and the share of the cigarette tax, levied nationally, which was assigned to municipalities in lieu of these excises proved generally inadequate. Town governments were therefore in poor shape financially, and any public improvements that were made came from special grants or loans from the central government.

1. The municipality of Athens, for example, had been insolvent for as long as anyone cared to recall. The problem was such that in 1955 and again in 1956, the Athens Power Company threatened to cut off the supply of electricity to municipal institutions unless some of the back bills were paid.

The Political Cosmos

However real the changes which had come in the senior ranks of the civil service and in local government, it remained true that plans for economic development and for most local improvements depended ultimately upon cabinet ministers who held office as politicians and not as economic or any other sort of technicians. Cabinet ministers in turn held their high positions at the pleasure of parliamentary deputies, whose votes depended partly on party affiliations, partly on personal ambition, and partly on calculations of the state of opinion among the electorate.

As in other countries where a managerial bureaucracy does not enjoy unchallenged control of the governmental machine, the issues that have most excited the politicians and the public in Greece have not been questions of economic policy and priority. Everyone is in favor of economic development, everyone is against inflation; everyone is in favor of better salaries and pensions, and everyone is against an unbalanced budget. In other words, political debate is not carried on in responsible economic terms, and a government in office always finds it impossible to live up to wild promises its leaders made in campaign speeches.

This sort of irresponsibility is by no means peculiar to Greece. Most politicians in democratic countries, not least in the United States, behave very similarly. What lends the Greek political world its peculiar character is the nature of the political parties and the irredentist tradition of Greek nationalism.

Political parties in Greece (with the exception of the Communist party) formed in the past around the person of a political leader rather than around a program or around local political machines. The system worked effectively only when an unusually gifted individual appeared on the scene, who, by the magnetism of his personality, was able to control his followers and keep them faithful to him. Eleftherios Venizelos was able to exert such leadership during parts of his career, though even he was not always successful. General Papagos achieved something similar during the first year or so when he held office, before his failing health raised the question of the succession and induced his followers to start jockeying for position.

When no single commanding figure was able to dominate the political scene — and this was normal — then political life became a complicated intrigue among ambitious individuals. Every cabinet spent a lot of energy smoothing over personal frictions within its own ranks, and attempting to block schemes, originating from the outside, to disrupt its following in the Chamber of Deputies. In many instances, these preoccupations prevented the cabinet from paying more than casual attention to the really important issues confronting Greece: questions of economic policy, in particular, were often neglected, and awkward decisions, bound to disappoint powerful individuals, were sometimes put off indefinitely.

The introduction of the majority system of election in 1952 was conceived, both by its Greek advocates and by the United States Embassy, as a promising remedy for this situation. The effect of the new electoral law was to compel separate personal parties to form election coalitions, since without a coalition no party could hope for a majority if any two others joined forces. But the coalitions did not really destroy the personal parties. Instead, the leaders forming a coalition bargained together to decide how many personal supporters each would be allowed to insert in the coalition's slate of candidates. Questions of the apportionment of cabinet positions and other honorific appointments, to be awarded in the event of victory, were also explored if not always settled in advance. To be sure, Papagos resisted this process and made few promises to the politicians who joined his Rally; yet even he, when it came to appointing his cabinet, rewarded the most conspicuous leaders of personal parties who had merged their following into his, by appointing them to ministerial positions.

By 1956, when the commanding personality of General Papagos had been removed from the scene, the actual differences made by the new electoral law were a good deal less marked than might at first appear. Under the old proportional electoral system, the critical negotiations to form a cabinet occurred after the elections; under the new majority system very similar negotiations preceded the elections. In either case, personal followings gathered around a specially conspicuous individual were the basic elements from which cabinets and coalitions were built. Even these building blocks of the political edifice were not very firm; a leader might find, almost overnight, that "his" followers had gone off after someone else who seemed to promise something new or different.

How a man became a party leader was hard to say. Very diverse personalities were active in Greek politics, and some party leaders seemed, at least from the outside, to have little personal impressiveness. Inheritance was a factor in some cases. Sophocles Venizelos, for example, had made his political career on the strength of his father's name, and on little else. Men who lacked such an advantage normally established leadership by oratory in the Chamber of Deputies and through newspaper publicity.

As the game of politics was played, the opposition regularly enjoyed certain advantages. This implied a degree of instability for any government. First of all, in any distribution of ministerial seats and other plums of office, more contenders were bound to be left out than could possibly be included. Efforts to solve this difficulty by enlarging the size of the cabinet have been made from time to time, but always at the cost of efficiency, since the more voices that have to reach agreement upon any policy, the more difficult it is to decide anything. Hence the size of Greek cabinets has fluctuated very markedly since World War II, from over twenty-five to less than fifteen members. But even when a cabinet was made unwieldy by the effort to include as many potential supporters as possible, there were always more disappointed than successful candidates; and to such discontented persons it was a standing temptation to break party lines and vote the government down in the Chamber of Deputies on any convenient issue. In the ensuing cabinet reshuffle they might always hope to do better, having proved their indispensability to the government by unseating it.

Second, the opposition was always in the position of being able to criticize without suggesting specific and practicable alternatives. It was easy to denounce half measures, to attack policies limited by the availability of money or of physical resources, to criticize the gaps between promises and actual achievements. The fact that much of what was thus attacked could not have been done much differently by anyone in power made little difference, since the opposition was not seriously concerned with what could or could not be done. Most politicians out of office were inclined to feel that any stick with which to beat the government, even a rotten one, was better than silence, so long as the stick hurt.

The irrelevance of much of the language of political debate to the real, underlying problems of Greek society was easy to criticize from the outside. Yet a sober technical discussion of what the government could and should accomplish, of relative priority among the many desirable projects, and of long-range policies calculated to relieve overpopulation and underemployment lacked all political appeal.

The difficulty was that Greece faced a formidable political-psychological problem. If large-scale investment on the basis of local resources were to occur, then restriction of current consumption would be necessary. Money and goods would have to be diverted from consumption to capital construction. Without such diversion, the country was condemned to chronic poverty, unless foreign investment and financing came to the rescue. Up to 1956 Greece had indeed depended upon foreign investment for its capital development; but the United States Congress could scarcely be counted upon to continue its support indefinitely. In fact, between 1954 and 1956 it became clear that American aid to Greece was to be shaped by more narrowly conceived American interests, which would mean that military subsidy and the disposal of surplus American agricultural products would take precedence over industrial or any other sort of capital investment in Greece. Moreover, a Greek government that depended upon American bounty would necessarily surrender a large portion of its effective sovereignty, as happened between 1947 and 1952. Such a policy would expose Greek authorities to charges of acting as craven "yes men" to the Americans, and of betraying Greek national interests, as, for instance, in Cyprus.

Dependence upon foreign funds to finance capital development was therefore a poor substitute for financing such development from local resources. Yet no one in Greece wanted to reduce and few wished to restrict the standard of living. The general public was impatient of austerity and wanted an immediate and miraculous increase in consumption levels. The chronic disbalance of the governmental budget reflected (among other factors) the pressure of these demands — demands for higher pensions and salaries, for better unemployment, medical and old-age benefits, and the like. To offer present hardship in the hope of future amelioration of economic conditions was therefore politically unthinkable, even though this was the only program that could really cope with the problems Greece confronted. Inflating the currency to pay current running expenses and to finance a modest program of government capital investment proved far more palatable politically, even though such a policy penalized the salaried and wage-earning classes, and led to recurrent crises as the price level outran their incomes.

Greece shares this problem with other underdeveloped nations in which population growth tends to equal or outstrip increases in productivity, while at the same time superficial contact with modern economic ideas has convinced leaders of public opinion that poverty is neither inevitable nor necessary, but can and should be relieved by government action. Under these circumstances, the processes of parliamentary government are most unlikely to turn up politicians who dare to contradict the immediate desire of the electorate for an improvement of living standards. Political irresponsibility toward fundamental economic problems, of a type so widespread in Greece, is a normal and all but inevitable result.

To 1956, at least, the discrepancy between the tenor of political debate and the planning of technicians in the economic ministries of the Greek government seems to have had only slight effect upon the practical realization of economic plans. In some cases, the fact that the minister was so often distracted by the exigencies of the political game may even have given civil servants a freer hand than they might otherwise have had. But if this was so, the major reason for it was the existence of the American aid mission, and the ultimate dependence of most economic advance upon grants from American authorities. That is to say, a senior civil servant, when confronted by his minister, could always point out that if his plans were not approved, then there might be a reckoning with the Americans, whose ideas about how the Greek government should try to shape the economy had much in common with the civil servant's approach, and little with that of the politicians.

It could almost be said that the Americans, having failed to alter the political pattern of Greece by direct intervention in 1950 and 1951, succeeded in short-circuiting the political process by dealing directly with the rising group of civil servants whose general outlook and whose personal positions in the hierarchy of administration had been profoundly influenced by the aid mission itself. This provided, temporarily at least, a workable substitute for responsible self-government; but it was an essentially fragile structure, depending both on the continuance of American grants to Greece and upon the acquiescence of the politicians.

Signs were not wanting in 1956 that the acquiescence of the politicians could not always be depended upon. Neutralism as between the Soviet Union and the United States had a few public advocates, and several newspapers systematically played up incidents that reflected discredit upon American personnel. There were also repeated newspaper attacks upon the privileged status American officials enjoyed. In the fall of 1955 popular demonstrations of sympathy for the Cypriotes in Athens, Salonika and Patras took a rather violent anti-American turn, including the stoning of American official buildings. Wherever I went in 1956 the inevitable question was put: Why does the United States not live up to its principles and support Greek claims in Cyprus?

In this indirect fashion, the Cyprus question allowed public expression of restiveness against American influence in Greece to assume a politically respectable, i.e., non-Communist, form. Part, though by no means a major part, of the emotional energy behind the Cyprus agitation in Greece reflected resentment against the American leading strings which had controlled Greece so thoroughly for nearly ten years.

Because the Cyprus question offered release for many diverse frustrations and grievances, it attained extraordinary proportions. All other political issues were in almost total eclipse in the summer of 1956. The opposition belabored the government for failing to free the Cypriotes; the government swore that no effort had been spared; and each side rivaled the other in denouncing the stubbornness of Britain, the meddling of Turkey and the indifference of the United States. Events in Cyprus, where nearly every day people were killed as a result of the guerrilla operations of an organization known by the initials EOKA (Ethniki Organosis Kypriakou Agonos, or National Organization of Cypriote Fighters), occupied the most prominent place in every newspaper, and speeches or statements about the Cyprus question filled an amazing proportion of the space that remained. Nothing else seemed to matter very much; and this attitude was not confined to newspapers. No conversation could long continue before the Cyprus question came up, and even very casual contacts between a Greek and an American were likely to produce an impassioned plea for Cyprus, together with reproaches against the United States government for failing to act in the matter.

From the point of view of someone interested in confronting and trying to relieve the economic and social difficulties of contemporary Greece, the Cyprus question was bound to appear totally irrelevant. If the Cypriotes were accorded the right to determine their own form of government, and if, as seemed overwhelmingly probab⁻e, the majority of the island's inhabitants then elected to unite with Greece, nothing would be helped so far as Greece's own problems were concerned. Yet by 1956 the liberation of Cyprus had become the very stuff and substance of Greek political debate. A more effective red herring would be difficult to imagine.

From the point of view of the Greek public, however, the Cypriote cause was sacred, and far more worthy of attention than merely economic questions. This attitude was deeply rooted in the political tradition of the nation. Indeed, the whole career of modern Greece, since the days when a small segment of the peninsula first won independence from the Turks, has been punctuated by recurrent bouts of intense popular excitement over the liberation of one or another portion of the Greek-speaking world that still remained under foreign sovereignty. In spite of costly failures, this agitation, and actions in accord with it, sooner or later added the Ionian Islands, Thessaly, Crete, Macedonia, the easterly Aegean Islands and part of Thrace to the Greek state. So successful has the nationalist program been that by 1956 Cyprus remained the only important area where a large Greek-speaking majority lived under foreign rule. The Greeks, therefore, felt entirely justified in demanding that such an anomaly end.

Anyone who takes democratic doctrines seriously must agree that the Greek case in Cyprus was a good one, since about 80 per cent of the islanders speak Greek and have given strong evidences of identification with Greece in recent years. Nor has the social and economic level of the Cypriotes been such as to justify a denial of self-government. Hence the Greeks of Greece had a good cause, and felt that the indifference of the United States to the issue, and the refusal of Britain to agree to grant self-government to Cyprus, represented a repudiation of their democratic professions. The burning conviction that the great powers were in the wrong and that the Greeks were in the right added fuel to the agitation, while Turkey's intervention in the question had the effect of opening once again all the wounds inflicted by past warfare between the two peoples.

On two occasions in the past, war with the Turks resulted from the desire of Greeks to liberate their fellow nationals, and on several other occasions war was narrowly averted by the intervention of the great powers. These wars and war scares cost Greece dearly in the past. One of the reasons for the failure of the economy to develop more rapidly was the financial burden the government incurred as a result of these enterprises; and the complete catastrophe which came to the Hellenic communities of Asia Minor in 1922 and 1923, following the failure of the Greek effort to annex part of the eastern Aegean coast, left marks upon the Greek body social which are still conspicuous. Yet then, as more recently in the case of Cyprus, counsels of caution or calculations of expediency scarcely found a hearing. The warm feeling of patriotism, all the warmer for being so reckless of consequences, overcame and continued to overcome every obstacle.

The Cyprus question became acute in the spring of 1955 when EOKA began issuing manifestoes and throwing bombs in the island, demanding self-determination and the end of colonial administration. Whether, or in what degree, the Greek government was an accomplice in provoking EOKA to action is impossible to say. Clandestine support of irregular armed action against a foreign government is an old tradition in the Balkans. The Greek government was itself attacked in this indirect fashion by Yugoslavia, Bulgaria and Albania during the guerrilla war; and all the Christian nations of the Balkans used similar methods against the Turks. The fact that the leader of EOKA was reputed to be Colonel George Grivas, a man who had once served in the Greek army, and who had been the head of an extra-legal rightist armed band in the years just after the end of World War II, suggested, but by no means proved, that agents of the Greek government may have had a hand in organizing the guerrillas in Cyprus.

If so (and this is not a proven fact), it seemed fairly clear that in the months that followed EOKA's appearance in Cyprus agitation in Greece grew to proportions that the government had not expected, and did not really desire. To have an issue upon which all Greeks could unite behind a government that boldly demanded justice for the Cypriotes was one thing; to have an issue that threatened to disrupt the NATO alliance in the eastern Mediterranean and gave the opposition a chance to attack the government for its inability to bring the situation to a satisfactory conclusion was quite another. Yet it was this second, embarrassing position into which the Greek government soon fell. The British refused to give in; and during the summer of 1955 the Turks began to assert their own interest in the fate of Cyprus.

Greece and Turkey had both been admitted to NATO in the fall of 1951, and in 1954 Greece had also concluded an alliance with Yugoslavia. This laboriously constructed diplomatic and military bulwark, within which Greece might hope to shelter as securely as any nation could that stood on the frontier between the Communist and non-Communist worlds, now began to crumble; and by 1956, although the treaties remained nominally in existence, the ill feeling between Greeks and Turks had reached a pitch that made real cooperation impossible. Joint naval maneuvers had to be called off, and acute difficulties arose in the NATO headquarters at Smyrna, where Greek and Turkish officers had been working side by side.

As this situation developed, the Greek government became seriously embarrassed. On the one hand, it could not allow the opposition to flaunt the garb of patriotism without challenge. The publicity agencies of the government and the Athens radio thereupon indulged in a veritable orgy of rhetoric which could not fail to have an inflammatory effect in Cyprus and also at home in Greece. On the other hand, rumor had it that the royal palace and the Foreign Office urged caution and moderation — a spirit which, however carefully it was kept under cover, still gave the opposition a chance to denounce the halfheartedness and secret duplicity of the government.

Through 1956 at least, the Greeks had spilled nothing more precious than words over Cyprus. The economic programs of the government had not been affected, nor had the social realities of Greece been touched. What had changed were Greek relations with Turkey and Britain; and in 1956 it was hard to see how the resultant damage to the NATO alliance could be repaired. A change in British policy might bring the Cypriotes self-determination and union with Greece — an upshot that would gratify the Greeks, but scarcely improve relations between Greece and Turkey. On the contrary, such an eventuality might well be accompanied by open violence between Turks and Greeks on Cyprus itself, where the Turkish minority constitutes about 20 per cent of the population; and similar and more dangerous disorders might spread into Turkish and Greek Thrace, where the two peoples remain mingled owing to the exclusion of this area from the exchange of populations that followed World War I.

The embitterment of Greek-Turkish relations seemed likely to endure for a long time, to the embarrassment of the Americans who wished to remain in alliance with both sides of the quarrel. It was, of course, because American diplomats dreaded such difficulties, and did not wish to antagonize the British, that the official policy of the United States remained so much aloof from the Cyprus question in 1955 and 1956.

Whatever the eventual outcome may be, it seems clear that the excitement over Cyprus had the effect not only of distracting attention from home policy, but also of weakening the Greek cabinet and restricting its freedom of maneuver. Feeling was directed most strongly against the Turks, secondly against the British, and more faintly but still definitely against the Americans. The emotional involvement with Cyprus was so strong that in the summer of 1956 it did not seem beyond the bounds of possibility that some turn of events in Cyprus might bring about the overthrow of the Karamanlis government and the installation of a cabinet far less inclined to cleave to the western alliance system of NATO in foreign affairs, and far less amenable to American advice concerning home policy.

What the effect of such a change might be upon the development of the economy, or upon the civil servants who were so busily planning its growth, cannot be forecast. My point merely is this: that the divorce between the realm of political discourse in Greece and the real problems of economic and social melioration within the nation is so wide as to be dangerous. Some economically ruinous action, rising from feelings of outraged nationalism, and provoked by politicians who hope to win place and prestige by risking everything on a politico-military gamble, may damage much of what has already been accomplished, or postpone indefinitely the realization of plans which have been laid for future economic expansion.

There are here the makings of a vicious circle. The major cause of the characteristic irresponsibility and extremism of Greek politics in recent decades, I am convinced, has been the chronic discontents and personal frustrations which tens of thousands of white-collar and professional people have felt. For them, politics offers a psychological release from daily difficulty and disappointment. To act as an adequate catharsis, political argument must be exciting, indeed inflammatory. The politicians therefore offer excitement, and when they cannot find it they try to manufacture it. If no internal foe seems sufficiently evil, then attacks are turned against some foreign antagonist. Political instability and changeability are the result, and when words boil over into actions real economic setbacks often follow — setbacks that feed the chronic discontent behind the political manifestations themselves.

Much of the domestic history of modern Greece can be interpreted as the result of such a vicious circle in action. The reconstruction of the economy and the transformation of the civil service since 1947 seem to offer a chance for escape from this circle, but escape is as yet by no means assured.

The Communist Problem

The Communist party was declared illegal in October 1947, and has remained illegal since then. Communist party leaders first joined the guerrillas, then retreated with the remnant of the guerrilla army behind the iron curtain. It seems entirely likely that the exile leadership was torn by faction and recrimination. Backwash from the shipwreck of their hopes on the Macedonian issue in 1949 must have continued to distract the secret councils of the party. Equally, the changing winds of doctrine that followed Stalin's death shook the Greek Communist party, and, combined perhaps with other factors, led in the fall of 1956 to the demotion of Nicholas Zachariades and the substitution of an almost unknown personality as Secretary General.

Rather strenuous police measures were taken during the guerrilla war to break up the Communist underground organization. Many people were arrested and several hundred were shot. How effective these measures were in breaking down the party organization cannot be judged by anyone standing outside the inmost party circles. Furthermore, the failure of the guerrilla enterprise, and the collision between Greek national feeling and international Communist policy over the question of the future of Macedonia must have disheartened even the most fanatical Communists in Greece, and certainly discredited Communism in the eyes of many who had formerly been sympathetic.

Whether these events mean that the Communist threat to Greece is lastingly removed, or whether the Greek Communist party will be able to rise once more from its defeat and become again a disciplined, dominating force in internal Greek politics, will depend at least as much upon the course of international affairs as upon any efforts the Greek Communists may make by themselves.

Nevertheless, in 1956 signs were not wanting to show that Communism was still a force to be reckoned with in Greece. In spite of all the police had been able to do, it seemed certain that an illegal underground organization continued to exist, aimed more, perhaps, at collecting intelligence for foreign Communist states than at fomenting revolution in Greece. Greek-language broadcasts from behind the iron curtain continued to reach the country, informing the faithful of the proper attitudes to take on current political questions. The fact has already been mentioned that one Athens newspaper faithfully followed the line laid down by Communist broadcasts; a second appeared most sympathetic, though its editors did not always conform completely to Soviet directives.

On the political stage, a new party was formed in advance of the elections of September 1951 which seemed very like EAM, the Communist-dominated resistance front which had so nearly won control of Greece in 1944. This new party was known by the initials EDA (Enosis Dimikratikon Aristera, or Union of the Democratic Left). Its candidates in 1951 were drawn in considerable measure from among persons who had made a name for themselves during the wartime resistance — many of them being in jail as Communists when the elections were held.

In spite of these circumstances, EDA met with very considerable success. In 1951 it won 180,640 votes, and in the elections of 1952, 152,011. In both cases, the EDA total was close to 10 per cent of all valid ballots, amounting to 10.6 per cent in 1951 and 9.6 per cent in 1952. Inasmuch as EDA participated in an electoral coalition with other opposition parties in the election of 1956, it is impossible to tell how many votes it may have contributed to the opposition's total on that occasion.

In 1951 and 1952, the defeat of the guerrilla army was still fresh and the demoralization of the Greek Communist party must have been serious. It therefore seems safe to assume that the proportion of about 10 per cent which EDA won in these elections represented about the minimal support the Greek Communist party commanded in the country. It is interesting to note, in passing, that a public opinion survey conducted by American and British experts in 1946 found 9.3 per cent of the population willing to declare to the faces of western interrogators an intention of following Communist instructions to abstain from the elections of that year. Very nearly the same proportion, and probably many of the same persons, supported EDA in 1951 and 1952. They must be regarded as "hard core" Communists or sympathizers so strongly attached to the party that nothing is likely to alienate them from Communist leadership.

Given the hardships under which many Greek families live and the history of the past fifteen years, during which on two separate occasions a Communist-led movement seemed on the verge of winning power, this proportion may appear satisfactorily, and even surprisingly, small. Many thousands of young people, after all, dedicated several years of their lives and underwent very real risks and discomforts in the service of a cause offered them by Communist propaganda. Such experiences and loyalties are not easily wiped out, especially when a person who has once been identified as a member of any sort of Communist organization is likely to suffer discrimination in job-hunting and in all contacts with the government forever after.

At the same time, a hard core of about 10 per cent of the voters constitutes a great political asset. It opens the door for deals with other parties and coalitions that may badly need just such support to win office. In 1956, the opposition coalition, under the leadership of George Papandreou, yielded to this temptation and accepted the proffered support of EDA. Papandreou was careful to announce, however, that in the event of victory he would not assign any seats in his cabinet to members of EDA; and after the election cooperation between EDA and Papandreou was promptly broken off.

Year in and year out, in the kaleidoscopic shifting of personal reputation that constitutes the warp and woof of Greek politics, it seems very doubtful whether any of the leaders of personal parties can regularly count on as much as 10 per cent of the vote. The apparently solid character of the Communist hard core thus takes on still greater significance. And in times when the discredit of the Communist party is not so recent as it was in 1951 and 1952, it seems at least possible that a fringe of fellow travelers and vague sympathizers — people who wish to protest vigorously against the status quo, and feel, quite correctly, that the Communists represent the most effective challenge to the prevailing social order — may add their votes to those of the hard core, and swell the proportion of the electorate responsive to Communist leadership quite considerably, perhaps to something like 20 per cent of the total.

This means, I believe, that the Communist problem has not been really solved. There still exists an important minority in the country which is prepared to go outside the framework of legality whenever opportunity offers a favorable prospect of success; a minority which on other occasions is ready to participate in the parliamentary process, to join electoral coalitions and to carry on newspaper campaigns against the government, but does all this fundamentally in bad faith, hoping to gain a toehold in the government only to convert it into a stranglehold, and then destroy the parliamentary machinery and civil liberty in favor of Communist dictatorship.

In 1956 these things were not apparent. Communism was not an issue; Cyprus had replaced it, and the Communist party had officially endorsed the Cyprus struggle over the radio. No one admitted to being a Communist, since to do so would have been a short way to jail. The people seemed quite genuinely glad to be relieved of the long preoccupation with the Communist question, and to find a cause upon which everyone could unite. This was, indeed, one of the reasons why Cyprus was such a heart-warming cause for the Greeks. Everyone, no matter what his opinions on domestic issues, was behind the Cypriotes. The Greeks had not known what it was to be united on an important public issue since the time of the Albanian war in 1940. Yet if Communists and nationalists were to quarrel in Cyprus, a possibility of which there were already some convincing signs in the summer of 1956, then the Communist question would emerge again in Greece with new bitterness, as each side sought to blame the other for the disruption of the Cypriote struggle.

In any analysis such as this it is easy to overemphasize the instability and insecurity of Greek political affairs. Certainly Greek politics are unstable, and the parliamentary regime in Greece is insecure. But it is well to remember that these conditions are not new. Exactly the same could be said of the political scene at any time since 1909, when the current phase of modern Greek political life began. The Greeks have learned to live with such conditions, and even manage to derive lively exhilaration from the perpetual uncertainty of their politics. Without politics, what would there be to talk about in the cafés?

The things that are new in Greek public life attract little public attention. The man in the street and in the village coffee house still takes pleasure in denouncing the inefficiency and stupidity of officialdom, and understands little if anything of the calculations and plans of the small group of civil servants who are busily trying to build a new future for the country. Their success is certainly not assured, but the fact that such men exist in the government opens the best prospect Greece has seen in more than a generation for the eventual attainment of social stability and secure economic progress. In the last chapter some observations will be made upon the probability of such an outcome.

CHAPTER 6

PROSPECTS FOR
SOCIAL STABILITY

If the fundamental reason for the erratic and occasionally violent course of recent Greek political life has been a serious disproportion between economic expansion on the one hand and population growth on the other — a view advanced in the preceding chapter — then it seems clear that since 1949 American aid and efforts of the Greeks to help themselves have sufficed to turn a critical corner. During the past six or seven years economic growth has definitely outstripped the increase of population. If these trends continue, Greece will be back on her feet economically after a few more years, and one can hope that the nation may then enter upon a period of internal social stability such as the people have not known for more than a generation.

Yet even by the rosiest calculations, some awkward years must lie ahead, during which important segments of the population will experience little of the growing prosperity of the country, and eager expectations of a better life will far outrun real possibilities. Prospects for the social stability of Greece hinge upon the question of what seems likely to happen during these critical years. A reasonably satisfactory economic life for all the inhabitants of the country can scarcely be foreseen in less than twenty years; and even if no internal distraction should interrupt the gradual processes of economic development during that period, there can be no guarantee that war or some other form of international disaster will not supervene to destroy part or all of what has been achieved.

Nevertheless, a real beginning has been made. This is clearly reflected in statistics of population and production. The birth rate is comparatively low — much lower than before the war — and the rate of population growth is declining steadily. The national product, on the other hand, is increasing much faster than the population, even though there are important fluctuations in the estimated gross national product from year to year, as a result mainly of variable weather affecting crop yields, but also because of changes in world prices for exported products.

Tables 1 and 2 show the magnitude of these changes. Thus, while the population grew by nearly half a million, or 6.6 per cent in the seven years between 1949 and 1955, the gross national product increased by 12,803 million drachmae, or 41.4 per cent.

Such figures are rather misleading, however. The year 1949 was a time of very unusual economic disorganization owing to the guerrilla war, and much of the increase in production that followed in the next two or three years was due to resumption of prewar activity. Moreover, the heavy inflow of American aid in the years between 1949 and 1952, which found expression in the extraordinary jump in gross national product for the year 1953 (when good weather also helped with the crops), makes the rate of growth during the first years covered by Table 2 irrelevant to any estimate of future probabilities.

A fairer appreciation of the long-range capacities of the Greek economy is to be gained if the period since 1953 alone is considered, when population has grown at nearly one per cent a year and production has increased on the average by a little more than 4 per cent a year. This ratio seems satisfactory enough. If production could be made to increase four times as fast as population for fifteen or twenty years, all would be well. There would then be enough new wealth in the country to drain the hill villages of their restless and superfluous young

TABLE 1

POPULATION, 1949–55

Year	Number	Annual Increase		Birth Rate per Thousand
		Number	Per Cent	
1949	7,482,748	n.a.	n.a.	18.6
1950	7,566,028	83,280	1.1	20.0
1951	7,653,611	87,583	1.2	20.3
1952	7,740,458	86,847	1.1	19.3
1953	7,824,303	83,845	1.1	18.4 [a]
1954	7,900,619	76,316	1.0	19.2
1955	7,972,744	72,125	.9	19.4

Source: National Statistical Services of Greece, Statistical Yearbook of Greece, 1955, Athens, 1956, Tables 8, 39.

a. This drop was attributed by Greek statistical authorities to a superstition against marriages in leap years (i.e., in 1952).

men, while for the town population satisfactory employment would be more and more easy to find.

But can this be done? What rate of economic growth can be maintained over the next fifteen to twenty years? The technical, fiscal and psychological possibilities are difficult to judge; but it seems obvious that continued expansion will require heavier and heavier investment in proportion to the increment of productivity achieved, if only because the easiest and most rewarding alternatives have, as a general rule, been exploited first. For example, doubling of crops by using fertilizers in the plains will never be possible again; the much more expensive method of irrigation will be needed to increase yields further in any-

TABLE 2

ECONOMIC PRODUCTION, 1949–55

Year	Agriculture	Industry	Gross National Product [a]	Annual Increase of GNP
	(Index: 1951 = 100)	(Index: 1951 = 100)	(Million Drachmae)	(Per Cent)
1949	n.a.	79	30,933	n.a.
1950	89	99	31,633	2.3
1951	100	100	34,346	8.6
1952	97	99	34,174	−.5
1953	124	116	40,170	17.5
1954	120	128	40,932	1.9
1955 (est.)	130	138	43,736	6.9

Source: U. S. Operations Mission/Greece, *Statistical Data Book,* Tables 136, 143.

a. Gross national product was calculated at market prices but adjusted to a stable cost level, as of 1951. *The Statistical Yearbook of Greece, 1955* (National Statistical Services of Greece, Athens, 1956), Table 193, offers a slightly divergent set of figures for the GNP, but the differences are so small as to be unimportant.

thing like the same proportion. Similar considerations apply with only slightly less force to other branches of production.

Nevertheless, official figures relating to consumption and investment show that the required heavier investment need not in itself prove crippling, for, in the years since 1949, a growing proportion of local production has been invested in fixed assets, while direct consumption has been increasing less rapidly than the national product. Table 3 reproduces the relevant statistics.

T A B L E   3

CONSUMPTION AND INVESTMENT, 1949–54
(*At 1951 Prices*)

Year	Consumption		Fixed Asset Formation		Gross National Product [a]	
	Amount	Annual Increase	Amount	Annual Increase	Amount	Annual Increase
	(*Million Drachmae*)	(*Per Cent*)	(*Million Drachmae*)	(*Per Cent*)	(*Million Drachmae*)	(*Per Cent*)
1949	30,277	n.a.	4,085	n.a.	30,933	n.a.
1950	30,605	1.1	5,861	43.5	31,633	2.3
1951	32,248	5.4	4,659	−20.5	34,346	8.6
1952	32,291	.1	4,275	−8.2	34,174	−.5
1953	36,103	11.8	4,947	15.7	40,170	17.5
1954	37,255	3.2	5,913	19.5	40,932	1.9

Sources: National Statistical Services of Greece, *Statistical Yearbook of Greece, 1955*, Athens, 1956, Tables 193, 195, and U. S. Operations Mission/Greece, *Statistical Data Book*, Tables 136, 143.

a. See Table 2, note a.

The most important fact revealed by Table 3, at least for present purposes, is the increasing margin between consumption and gross national product. In 1949 the difference was only 656 million drachmae, or 16.1 per cent of the total investment in fixed assets made in that year. The balance had to come, of course, from foreign aid. By 1954, however, the margin between consumption and production had risen to 3,677 million drachmae, or 62.2 per cent of the investment in fixed assets made in that year.

All this appeared very encouraging. The use made of domestic savings was scarcely satisfactory, however. They went very largely into housing, while investment in more economically productive enterprises lagged and in some cases even declined in absolute volume. From the figures in Table 4 it

TABLE 4

FIXED ASSET FORMATION, 1949–54

(*Million Drachmae at 1951 Prices*)

Year	Total	Housing	Agriculture	Manufactures	Transport and Communication	Electricity and Gas	Mining
1949	4,085	1,347	444	456	1,025	109	7
1950	5,861	1,817	606	858	1,427	161	71
1951	4,659	1,404	566	712	671	538	187
1952	4,275	1,351	361	740	506	402	121
1953	4,947	1,706	364	492	729	618	74
1954	5,913	1,905	416	456	1,179	876	58

Source: National Statistical Services of Greece, *Statistical Yearbook of Greece, 1955,* Athens, 1956, Table 195.

appears that from 1949 to 1954 about one third of all investment in Greece took the form of housing, whereas, after the withdrawal of large-scale American aid, the rate of investment in manufacturing, mining and agriculture tended to decrease. Until 1953, when a renewed road-building program was introduced by the government (largely as a device for relieving unemployment), the pattern of investment in transport and communication followed the same declining curve.

This distribution of capital resources does not seem wise. Greek government economists were keenly aware of the situation and very much desired to channel more investment into industry. The difficulty was that the public preferred brick and mortar, distrusted banks, and kept a large proportion of its liquid capital in gold coins. Possibly the official manipulators of the economy will succeed in luring private funds into the open, so to speak, and be able to divert a larger proportion into industrial or other forms of productive investment in future years. Up to 1956 there was little sign that this was being achieved; yet if something of the sort does not occur it seems unlikely that the growth of production will long continue at the rate which prevailed during the recent past. Even so, an average annual increase of the national product by only 2 or 3 per cent would be enough to keep productivity ahead of population, and permit a gradual lifting of living standards.

Population trends are working very definitely to simplify the task of economic planners. Families are becoming smaller. The census of 1920 showed an average family household of 4.29 persons; by 1940 this figure had shrunk to 4.25, and by 1951 to 4.11. [1]

This phenomenon may have been due in part to a growing use of contraceptives, especially in towns, but this factor was probably not of great importance. A profound and pervasive shyness surrounds the whole subject of birth control in Greece, and definite information on the subject was impossible to find. Probably more important in restricting the size of families, and certainly more accessible to measurement, is the tendency to postpone marriages. The increase in the percentage of single persons since 1907 is shown in Table 5. These figures are affected by a change in the sex ratio of the population, which in

1. National Statistical Services of Greece, *Statistical Yearbook of Greece, 1955,* Athens, 1956, Table 34.

1907 showed a small excess of males, and in 1951 a 1.2 per cent excess of females. Nevertheless, the critical change can clearly be seen in the growing proportion of women who do not marry until after the age of thirty. The figures for 1907 may be taken as representative of the situation that prevailed when old-fashioned peasant customs still reigned almost unchallenged in Greece; and it is interesting to notice that a strong tendency to postpone the age of marriage was apparent by 1920, only to be set back by the more reckless habits of the refugee population, reflected in the census of 1928, and then resumed and carried to further lengths by 1951.

On the strength of these figures, and on the evidence earlier cited of changes in family customs, it seems safe to forecast a continuation of the decline in the rate of population growth for a good many years to come. Indeed, it would not be surprising if some twenty or thirty years from now population growth halted entirely and a decline set in, at least among the peasantry. If the family customs so strikingly exemplified in Nea Eleftherohori spread and become general among the rural population so that marriages become tied to a large dowry and

TABLE 5

PERCENTAGES OF SINGLE PERSONS, CENSUS YEARS 1907, 1920, 1928, 1951

Census Year	Women			Men		
	20–30	30–40	40 and Over	20–30	30–40	40 and Over
1907	12.4	4.4	3.9	28.0	12.3	7.9
1920	17.6	4.7	3.1	30.1	12.7	7.2
1928	16.2	5.0	3.6	28.2	11.3	6.9
1951	21.1	7.6	4.8	31.8	12.5	6.6

Source: National Statistical Services of Greece, *Statistical Yearbook of Greece, 1955*, Athens, 1956, Table 25.

dependent upon calculations of the potential standard of living available to the new family, then, in a time when expectations of a higher standard of living are strong, depopulation of seriously overcrowded rural areas will become automatic. The demographic history of rural Ireland in the past century illustrates what may yet occur in Greece (and perhaps in other peasant countries of eastern Europe as well), although the Irish retreat from rural overpopulation was of course enormously facilitated by emigration overseas, on a scale which is no longer possible for the peasants of Greece or of eastern Europe generally. [2]

All these statistics show, in my opinion, that Greece has at least made a good start toward bringing developed resources into a better balance with the country's population. Even if, as seems probable, the recent rate of expansion of production slows down a bit, nevertheless it will gradually become possible to improve living standards and to satisfy, better than before, the economic aspirations of the population. This, it seems to me, is as much as could be asked of the American economic aid program: A tendency for population to outstrip production has been reversed, and government officials have been trained to watch for and plan against any threatened return of the old unhappy situation. From this point of view, one can properly assert that the aid programs have been a success.

Two criticisms may nevertheless be made of policies and achievements to date. One is that little attention seems to have

2. For an account of the change in marriage habits which lay behind the depopulation of modern Ireland, see Conrad M. Arensberg, *The Irish Countryman,* Macmillan, New York, 1937, and Conrad M. Arensberg and Solon T. Kimball, *Family and Community in Ireland,* Harvard University Press, Cambridge, 1940. Parallels between Irish developments and the recent changes in Greek peasant marriage customs are quite striking, and it may be that Ireland's demographic history represents the earliest and in our time the most advanced instance of a pattern of development that may assert itself widely in the agrarian parts of the world during the next century.

been paid to long-term calculations of the level of development at which to aim. Should Greece aspire to become a highly industrialized state with a technically advanced agriculture and elaborate service occupations? Should the country strive to become another Switzerland? Or is the Danish pattern more practicable? Should specialized agriculture for an international market play the leading role, and industry come second?

The Greeks themselves, as well as American experts who have been concerned with Greek development, have definitely tended to prefer the first alternative, giving industrialization priority, and aiming for the maximum. This is natural enough. Modern industry has great prestige in the thoughts and feelings of people who live in underdeveloped lands today. It seems like a talisman to national wealth and power, since it was largely through industrial strength that the great powers of the earth attained their greatness during the last century or more. Yet it is a moot point whether large-scale industry can really be made to flourish in Greece without far-reaching changes in the psychological and social patterns of the nation, not to speak of the technical problems presented by raw material shortages and the relatively high cost even of domestically produced power.

The technical difficulties could perhaps be overcome — at least in an ideally rational world where atomic energy and efficient transportation might be made (for irrational, i.e., nationalistic reasons) to bring the factors of industrial production to the labor force instead of allowing the labor force to congregate at the most favorable sites. But the psychological and social patterns which have hitherto obstructed the free development of large-scale industry in Greece — particularly the force of the family in-group that cuts across and interferes with larger loyalties to more impersonal associations required by industrial technology — these patterns are a good deal more difficult to deal with, even in a completely rational world. The multitude of factors which combine to make men and nations what they are, are certainly not understood by anyone, and deliberate efforts to change them are unlikely to be very successful when such understanding is absent. Nor even if the necessary knowledge were at hand, would a man who valued human dignity and individuality be likely to welcome social management of an all-encompassing sort, capable of making over value systems and family systems in the interest of greater economic efficiency.

While I would not wish to suggest that the efforts to build up modern industry in Greece should therefore be given up, it does seem to me that a greater emphasis on the development of rural cooperatives, more financial and technical help in matters of marketing, grading, food processing, and more effort to open foreign markets for fruits and vegetables — fresh, frozen, canned or dried — might bring far greater returns for a much smaller investment than can, under present circumstances, come from building technically up-to-date factories. But such a program is less spectacular, less appealing, even though — or perhaps just because — it lies closer to the traditional strengths of Greek enterprise, in the fields of trade and merchandising.

An objection against such an emphasis is that if Greece were to become dependent upon distant markets for perishable and easily dispensable commodities, then the vulnerability of the economy to any disturbance of international trade would be dangerously great. This cannot be denied. Greece is already dangerously vulnerable to any upset of international markets, since her exports are largely luxury or semi-luxury goods and her imports embrace prime necessities. To accentuate this vulnerability in a world where international relations are precarious might therefore seem a path with little to recommend it. This has certainly been one of the calculations lying behind the Greeks' preference for industrial development.

On the other hand, Greek industry has not been able, hitherto, to compete with the more industrially advanced countries

in international markets, and it is difficult to imagine a time
when Greek industry will be able to compete successfully in
world markets on any large scale. A vigorous industry to serve
the internal market of the country obviously depends on the
purchasing power of the population at large, especially the
rural population, which still constitutes the majority. The most
immediate way to raise the purchasing power of the farmers is
surely to organize intensive market gardening more widely,
that is, to embark upon the precarious but potentially rewarding path of regional agricultural specialization, supplying markets of northern Europe.

In my opinion, therefore, the Danish pattern deserves more
attention in Greece, and smaller-scale enterprises for processing
and marketing labor-intensive crops, whether cooperatively or
privately owned, should receive more official encouragement
and financial help, while grandiose plans for industry should
take second place. To plan upon war or depression is, for a
country like Greece, to anticipate paralyzing disaster in any
event. To take the risk involved in becoming an agriculturally
specialized area would therefore seem worth while, however
serious that risk may be.

A second important question which official planning has not
really explored is control of population. This has two aspects:
prevention of unwanted births by contraceptives, and removal
of unemployable surplus population through emigration. Both
have been left entirely in private hands. This is not surprising,
for economic development was, until very recently, considered
a wholly private matter. Yet if the central problem of the country is the ratio between population and developed resources,
there can be no theoretical justification for confining public policy to the second half of the ratio only.

To be sure, there are powerful psychological reasons for doing so, and when population phenomena are but little understood, even by experts, it is perhaps wise for governments to

refrain from making efforts to limit population growth by heavy-handed invasion of a realm that is still private all around the world. On the other hand, it cannot be denied that public health services, by keeping more people alive, act, in a country like Greece, to accentuate economic difficulties. Moreover, the device which private initiative has found for limiting births — the postponement of marriage — puts great psychological strain upon young people, who are compelled to forego what they still feel is a normal right in order to maintain an economic status which is in itself scarcely satisfactory to them.

Neither the Greek Orthodox Church, to which almost the entire population of the country adheres, nor state authorities have ever taken any sort of position upon birth control. A private association, known as the Eugenic Society, was organized in 1952 for the purpose of spreading information about contraceptives; but in view of the general taboo upon any sort of public discussion of these matters, this body has remained most discreet, and has systematically avoided publicity for any of its activities. This is as far as public policy seems to have gone with respect to control of population through limitation of births.

Emigration, on the other hand, has attracted considerable attention in Greece, mostly unfavorable. Newspapers, and spokesmen for the armed services of the country, have deplored the loss of those young men who were able to work their way through the various barriers to free migration which modern governments have erected. There is a widespread feeling, especially among army officers, that Greece needs numbers in order to stand off the Slavic threat in the north. If this implies grinding peasant poverty, so much the worse; but numbers are essential.

This attitude seems very shortsighted to me. Even in war, a relatively small but reasonably well educated and technically proficient soldiery is likely to outmatch brute numbers, especially if the living conditions under which brute numbers languish are such as to breed discontent with the social order and distrust of those in authority. The sort of thinking that seems to prevail in the Greek army reflects a time when a single man with a rifle or machine gun was the unit of combat, rather than teams of rather highly trained men serving complicated machines: airplanes, tanks, radios, trucks and the like.

Even though the conditions of localized Balkan warfare may not have changed so very radically from rifle and machine gun days, it would still be true that manpower chronically disaffected toward the social and political system they are expected to defend would be worse than useless. A poverty-stricken and discontented peasantry, no matter how numerous, would be more of a liability than an asset to the military strength of Greece.

There seems, therefore, no reason why the Greek government should not encourage emigration, and use its diplomatic agents to try to facilitate the movement of young people overseas. Certainly emigration is the shortest and most effective of all possible ways to relieve unemployment. A man who might easily become a Communist in Greece, living on the margins of society, would, in a richer and more prosperous environment, be able to find a satisfactory life for himself and become a good citizen of his adopted country. More than this, emigrants have regularly sent large sums of money to their relatives back home; in fact, emigrant remittances have long constituted an important item in the nation's balance of payments. As the generations pass, these remittances will inevitably shrink, unless fresh emigration renews the stream. From the point of view of the Greek government, no easier way to earn foreign exchange could be imagined; from the point of view of the American government, one young man admitted to the United States from Greece easily equals $10,000 spent in Greece for economic development.

The neglect of emigration as a device to ease the Greek economic problem seems to me the greatest weakness of both Greek and American policy, since in no other way can so much advantage be gained so quickly and so cheaply. In spite of the prejudice against migration on both sides, I am convinced that a flow of 5,000 to 10,000 persons annually from Greece to the United States would bring nothing but gain to both countries.

The Greek government, it should be pointed out, has not prevented emigration, although it has made it difficult for young men of military age to leave the country. Some countries — notably Australia, Canada, Brazil and Venezuela — have admitted comparatively large numbers of Greeks since the war, and even the United States set up a special program in 1953 which allowed the immigration of several thousand persons in excess of the normal Greek quota of slightly more than 300 a year. Since many Greeks are eager to leave the country, the result of these measures was to make emigration a significant factor in the Greek demographic balance, as Table 6 shows.

TABLE 6

MIGRATION OF GREEK CITIZENS, 1947–55

Year	Arrivals	Departures	Net Emigration
1947	20,317	34,030	13,713
1948	22,932	31,677	8,745
1949	21,077	24,943	3,866
1950	30,870	34,937	4,067
1951	44,120	58,626	14,506
1952	55,265	62,810	7,545
1953	56,306	67,071	10,765
1954	71,815	94,743	22,928
1955	78,172	111,597	33,425

Source: National Statistical Services of Greece, Statistical Yearbook of Greece, 1955, Athens, 1956, Table 41.

When one remembers that since the resumption of statistical services after the end of the guerrilla war the annual increase in population varied between a maximum of 87,583 in 1951 and a minimum of 72,125 in 1955, it becomes clear that emigration, in spite of the indifference of the Greek government and the ambivalence of American authorities, has in fact played an important part in slowing the growth of population in Greece, thereby significantly relieving economic pressure upon those who remained behind.

The criticisms I have made of the economic policies pursued by Greek and American authorities are perhaps academic. Policy, after all, has to be worked out in a political environment, and must take account of biases and prejudices as well as of theoretical possibilities and limits. Still, I feel that some official efforts might have been made to educate opinion to favor, or at least to tolerate, population planning as well as economic planning, and to consider the rewards of agricultural specialization as against what may be somewhat premature industrial development. Nor should my remarks obscure the central fact that during the past six years, in spite of the very great handicaps inherited from nine years of war and political disturbance, the economy of Greece has been put upon a basis that promises an eventual solution for most of the crying difficulties the country has faced internally for fifty years or longer.

In any attempt to assess the probabilities of social stability in Greece, however, one must not forget the problems which have not been solved, and which could not have been solved by any wisdom or skill on the part of the American aid mission or of the Greek government.

One of these problems is the unequal impact of economic advance upon different segments of the population of Greece. This has been emphasized in preceding chapters, but the matter is so important as to bear repetition: As long as the effect of agricultural improvement is to enrich the farmers of the plains while doing little or nothing for the shepherds, woodcutters and part-time farmers in the hills, then a renewal of guerrilla action will remain a possibility; and as long as economic expansion continues to be financed in significant proportion by inflation of the currency, so that those who own physical goods prosper while those who sell their labor suffer, an analogous exacerbation of social tensions within urban communities must be expected. Statistics proving over-all advance are all very well, but if important and strategically located segments of the population have reason to feel resentful at being left out, economic progress must remain precarious. How precarious will depend on the numbers, organization and will to action of the discontented minority; and since the Communists in Greece have a traditional tie with rural hillsmen and with urban workmen based upon the wartime resistance and the postwar guerrilla movement, it would be foolish to suppose that organization or will to action, even violent action, is likely to be lacking for long.

I must confess that I can see no way in which these difficulties can be solved speedily, or even significantly relieved in the near future, as long as one considers only what can be done within Greek frontiers. To be sure, a more rigorous monetary policy might reduce or even stop inflation, but this would also reduce or stop investment, thus postponing the long-term solution to Greek economic difficulties in the interest of greater social cohesion and stability in the short run. How can one weigh these contradictory desiderata? In 1956 the American aid mission was emphasizing caution and the dangers of inflation; the Greek civil servants of the economic ministries were emphasizing investment and the dangers of standing still economically. Just where the path of wisdom lies, I, at least, do not feel able to say.

Similarly, how can the misery of the hill villages be relieved until towns and plains become even richer and begin to need more labor? Migration from the hills seems to offer the only adequate solution for villages like Cherasia. But migration within Greece is pointless until there are jobs, and jobs for strangers can open up only after the surplus labor already at hand has been absorbed into a growing economy. This, indeed, is where overseas migration once played a saving role, and where it might do so again if more effort were made to enlarge opportunities. Hill communities have an old tradition of emigration; hillsmen, having least to leave behind, are still the most ready to depart. But if we think only of the Greek scene, and neglect, as Greek and American authorities hitherto have neglected, the possibility of achieving and maintaining some optimum flow of migration (so far as I know, the very concept of an optimum migration rate has never been entertained), then it is hard to deny that the hills must wait for relief until after the plains and towns of Greece have raised their prosperity considerably above existing levels. Under such circumstances the risk that the men in the hills will become impatient and refuse to wait peaceably must simply be endured.

The second great problem confronting Greece is even more stubborn and most assuredly cannot be solved within Greek frontiers. This is the utter vulnerability of Greece to war or economic depression. It is all too clear that there is little the Greeks can do by themselves to ward off or reduce these dangers to their society.

It does not need argument to prove that the outbreak of war between the great powers of the world would almost certainly involve Greece, and would be very likely to erase much or all of the economic progress which recent years have brought. The threat of such a war already involves a very heavy burden for the Greek economy; and without continued American aid the armed forces of Greece cannot be maintained at anything like their existing size and level of equipment. Military pay, pensions and expenditures for military installations already constitute about one third of the Greek government's budget; and active military operations, even on a small scale, would speedily disrupt Greek finances and interrupt economic progress.

This is, however, a danger that Greece shares with most of the world. Her geographical position, abutting directly upon the Communist area of eastern Europe, makes the danger only a little more acute than it is for countries farther away from the front lines. The same might be said of the danger from international economic depression. No country of the free world could easily endure a repetition of the experiences of the 1930's, and Greece less than most because of the fragility of her economy and society.

The progress of the economic programs in Greece has somewhat reduced national dependence upon foreign supplies. The new electricity grid, for example, draws its power resources from within the country and makes imported fuel less vital than before; and the increases in the crops of wheat and other food grains mean that a smaller proportion of the basic food supply of the nation has to come from abroad. But by no stretch of the imagination can Greece hope to become self-sufficient economically; and the general bias of her export trade in favor of highly priced semi-luxury items of agricultural origin cannot be altered quickly, even if it should seem wise to try to do so.

If war or depression should come, therefore, the economic and social processes which now promise an eventual solution to the chronic poverty of Greece would be reversed. Some future generation would then be presented with the task of picking up whatever pieces survived from the social fabric as it now exists, and trying to put them together into a workable whole once more.

Even short of such ultimate disasters, Greek economic expansion is still a tender and weakly rooted plant, which has not yet really begun to flourish beyond the confines of a greenhouse erected by foreign aid. If the inflow of foreign funds were to stop, most of the presently scheduled investment programs would stop too, or at least would have to be drastically curtailed. If adverse international economic conditions came to prevail, so that blocked exchanges, national austerity programs, tariffs and other protective devices became more prevalent than they are today, this, too, would threaten the financial position of Greece and might blast the prosperity of the farmers raising crops for export.

These dangers are real enough, and no one can confidently predict that what has been so laboriously attained in the past few years may not be lost in as many months. Yet this is a universal penalty for technical and commercial advance. The more fully and rationally Greece exploits her special resources, the more completely the nation becomes dependent upon the smooth operation of complex and potentially fragile marketing arrangements. A village that raises almost everything its members need may be poor, but it is at least secure against all but immediate local disaster; a village that raises products to be consumed thousands of miles away is likely to be far more prosperous and to enjoy goods far more abundant and satisfactory than those that could be provided locally, but its security has been lost.

Greece cannot aim at local self-sufficiency of the age-old peasant pattern. There are too many mouths to feed for that to be possible any longer. Integration into a far larger economy, extending far beyond the limits of the Greek state, is imperative, and has long been so. This brings with it the dangers mentioned as well as rewards which the Greeks have begun to glimpse. If the adventure fails as a consequence of international disorder, then depopulation of the sort that visited Kotta between 1947 and 1949 is the horrible specter that rises over the entire nation. If the venture succeeds, one can foresee, after another generation or so, a far more attractive picture: a Greece comparatively prosperous, with a population generally contented, enjoying a political life markedly less flamboyant than that which now prevails.

In which of these directions Greece will move cannot be foretold. Human affairs have not usually been governed by reason and are never divorced from hot passions and high affections. Setbacks to processes of social, economic and political integration have been frequent, and are especially conspicuous in the history of the Balkan peninsula. Yet for all the destructive power of war, the devastation of disease and the damages of civil violence, the general course of human history has been progress toward ever higher levels of integration. This progress has certainly not been steady. The movement resembles instead the waves of a rising tide, reaching new levels only to recede and then advance once more.

The recent history of Greece represents, in my view, an effort in the direction along which human development has been going for several thousand years. This does not mean that success is assured; it does mean that we should wish Greece well, and hope that neither the domestic nor the foreign dangers that beset her will succeed in checking or destroying the enrichment of the country through a progressively more exact articulation of her economic energies and resources into a trans-national — and eventually into a world-wide — market.

Such hopes have at least this basis to rest upon: If trends of the last ten years continue for the next twenty, then most of the internal problems that now make Greek life so precarious will have sunk to insignificance, and Greek society will be able to confront the rest of the world internally stable and strong. Luck and tact, patience and wisdom, on the part of the Greeks and on the part of the greater nations of the world, will all be needed if this result is to be achieved; but the changes that can bring such a happy solution to Greece's recent troubles are under way. This was not true ten years ago or even eight years ago. Greek and American effort has made the difference. It is no mean achievement; it is one in which both nations may properly take pride.

APPENDICES

UNITED STATES AID TO GREECE, 1947–56

(*Millions of Dollars Appropriated*)

Fiscal Year June 30 — July 1	Economic Aid	Military Aid	Annual Total	Cumulative Total
1947–48	230.2	197.8	428.0	428.0
1948–49	243.1	147.5	390.6	818.6
1949–50	287.4	131.5	418.9	1,237.5
1950–51	284.4	150.7	435.1	1,672.6
1951–52	181.0	n.a.	n.a.	n.a.
1952–53	80.6	n.a.	n.a.	n.a.
1953–54	21.3	n.a.	n.a.	n.a.
1954–55	41.9	n.a.	n.a.	n.a.
1955–56	66.7	n.a.	n.a.	n.a.

Sources: U. S. Operations Mission/Greece, *Statistical Data Book*, Table 49; data for 1955–56 from U. S. Information Service press release, April 27, 1956.

BALANCE OF PAYMENTS, 1950–55
(*Million Drachmae*)

	1950	1951	1952	1953	1954	1955
Exports	1,701	1,845	2,192	4,418	6,066	7,570
Invisible income	552	650	741	1,947	2,472	3,081
Total current receipts	2,253	2,495	2,933	6,365	8,538	10,651
Imports	6,958	6,498	5,712	7,900	10,670	12,390
Invisible payments	64	48	44	104	94	177
Total current payments	7,022	6,546	5,756	8,004	10,764	12,567
Current deficit	4,769	4,051	2,823	1,639	2,226	1,916
Capital transfers to Greece (U. S. aid, reparations, loans)	4,343	4,378	1,881	1,219	1,752	2,331
Net balance	–426	327	–942	–420	–474	415

Source: National Statistical Services of Greece, *Statistical Yearbook of Greece, 1955,* Athens, 1956, Table 182.

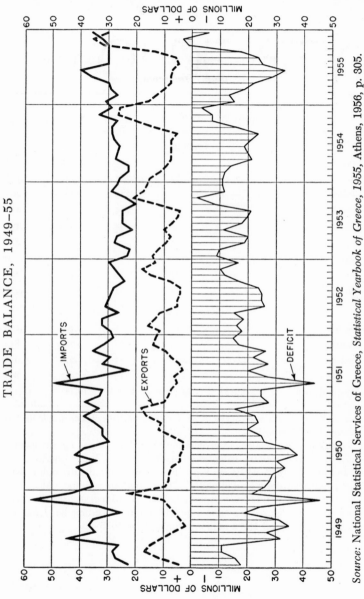

APPENDIX 3

TRADE BALANCE, 1949–55

Source: National Statistical Services of Greece, *Statistical Yearbook of Greece, 1955,* Athens, 1956, p. 305.

APPENDIX 4

STATE BUDGET OF GREECE, 1951–56
(*Million Drachmae*)

	1951–52	1952–53	1953–54	1954–55	1955–56 (est.)
		Income			
Direct taxes	1,295	1,551	1,833	2,202	2,035
Indirect taxes	3,792	4,072	5,367	6,146	7,345
Domestic loans	—	—	229	217	400
Public investments	—	42	195	251	150
Other domestic revenue	635	646	1,034	1,025	1,335
U. S. aid	17	683	1,457	1,202	1,400
Foreign credits	—	—	—	120	30
NATO	—	28	49	392	225
Total income	5,739	7,021	10,164	11,554	12,919
		Expenditure			
Civil ministries	4,056	3,993	5,048	6,100	7,298
Public security	515	575	668	729	830
War ministries	2,000	2,020	2,625	2,971	3,050
Other	41	45	229	532	861
Total expenditure	6,612	6,632	8,570	10,331	12,039

Source: National Statistical Services of Greece, *Statistical Yearbook of Greece, 1955*, Athens, 1956, Table 196.

Note: Owing to complications of accounting procedures, these figures incorporate some anomalies. Only certain categories (mainly military) of American aid are counted, and prior to 1953–54 Italian reparations were omitted, although reparations from other countries were included under "Other domestic revenue." Moreover, the state investment budget was kept separately. The *Statistical Yearbook of Greece, 1955* gives only two figures for state expenditures on investments: 1,397 million drachmae for 1954–55 and 1,472 million estimated for 1955–56.

CURRENCY AND CREDIT, 1947–55

Year (as of December)	Currency Circulation	Bank Loans Outstanding	Economic Development Financing Organization Loans (U. S. Aid to Industry) Outstanding
	(*Million New Drachmae*)		(*Million Dollars*)
1947	974	n.a.	—
1948	1,202	2,074	—
1949	1,859	3,388	10.3
1950	1,887	4,560	38.0
1951	2,199	5,612	67.0
1952	2,476	5,428	75.6
1953	3,503	5,978	77.7
1954	3,888	8,036	72.1
1955	4,951	8,433	76.4

Source: National Statistical Services of Greece, *Statistical Yearbook of Greece, 1955,* Athens, 1956, Tables 199, 200.

COST OF LIVING INDEX IN ATHENS, 1950–55
(*1952 = 100*)

Year	General	Food	Clothing	Housing
1950	84.5	90.1	76.1	46.9
1951	95.1	95.7	94.8	75.0
1952	100	100	100	100
1953	109.0	107.8	104.9	175.0
1954	125.4	121.1	126.4	180.0
1955	132.6	125.9	130.7	255.0

Source: National Statistical Services of Greece, *Statistical Yearbook of Greece, 1955,* Athens, 1956, Table 213.

INDEX

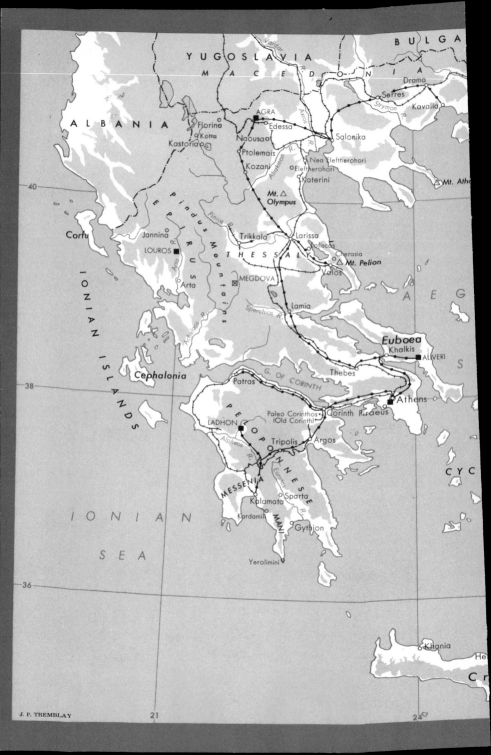